UNIVERSITY OF AMSTERDAM

A MINIGRAPH

University of Amsterdam: a minigraph

FifthMan,
c/o Allford Hall Monaghan Morris
Morelands, 5-23 Old Street
London EC1V 9HL
UK

ISBN 978-0-9934378-8-5

First published in 2019 by FifthMan.

Editor: Emma Keyte

THIS IS THE STORY OF A DESIGN COMPETITION WIN WHICH LED TO A TWELVE-YEAR PROJECT TO REMODEL THE UNIVERSITY OF AMSTERDAM'S UNCOMPLETED POST-WAR CAMPUS. AS A RESULT, A SERIES OF EXISTING BUILDINGS, MEGASTRUCTURAL IN SCALE, HAS BEEN KNITTED BACK INTO THE FINER FABRIC OF THE DUTCH CAPITAL'S STREET AND CANAL SYSTEMS, AND A DISPARATE RANGE OF NEW LEARNING SPACES CONSOLIDATED INTO A COHERENT AND LEGIBLE FORM.

IT'S ALSO THE STORY OF AN ATTITUDE TO DESIGN, AN ATTITUDE THAT ACKNOWLEDGES THE COMPLEXITY OF THE BRIEF AND THE LIKELIHOOD OF IT CHANGING OVER TIME BY SUGGESTING A ROBUST SET OF PRINCIPLES: A FLEXIBLE STAGE SET OF SPACES ESTABLISHED WITHIN THE CITY AND CAMPUS THEATRE THAT IS THEN FURTHER PERSONALISED BY PROPS ACCORDING TO THE ACADEMIC PROGRAMME.

TIME AND THE CITY CAMPUS

SALOMÉ A. BENTINCK

Innovation is key to academia, but strangely enough our image of famous old universities, like Cambridge and Oxford, tends to be one of unchanging tradition. This paradox is also found in Amsterdam where the far younger University of Amsterdam (UvA) has its origins in the inner city. Here too, one can find old buildings that breathe an atmosphere of history and tradition: ancient cloisters and yards and nineteenth-century hospitals. This ambivalent relationship between academia and change fascinates me both as an architect and as a client.

Change came to universities when expansion became necessary to accommodate the children of the post-war baby boom. New ideas and insights about education and science demanded new types of buildings. Campuses that were built in the sixties express these new insights and the great visions of the post-war world: humanity, science and youth. They were large modernist buildings, the design led by their function. If possible, all buildings were conveniently connected above ground level. The UvA site at Roeterseiland in Amsterdam, designed by Norbert Gawronski, was one such campus. It was built without any sentimentality towards the surrounding neighbourhoods, in accordance with the major municipal interventions of the day. However, Roeterseiland remained unfinished. Following the Paris uprisings of 1968, students, staff and citizens felt empowered to protest together against the municipality's plans for the large-scale demolition of some Amsterdam neighbourhoods. What followed was a reappraisal of old urban structures, with their cosiness and humane scale.

One might expect that the more corporate university management style introduced in the eighties and nineties would have resulted in educational buildings in glassy high-rises. But the heritage status of the inner city and the activism of both citizens and the university population meant this didn't happen in Amsterdam. In fact, the corporations were influenced by the universities. The attractions of the traditional campus were discovered by corporate developers, who inflated the concept of the 'business campus' into a brand-new selling point.

In the meantime, the visions of the sixties, solidified into brutal concrete, neither matched the evolving academic identity of the university, nor contributed to the urban context. So what to do with these remains? Demolish or refurbish?

The attractiveness of cities like Amsterdam caused extra growth in (international) student numbers, growth that could easily have generated 'education factories'. The university was criticised for being inhuman and too corporate. Citizens saw the university as a juggernaut, too self-contained, but causing a lot of bustle and nuisance. Demolition of the sixties campus at Roeterseiland might have been in line with prevailing attitudes, but it would not have been an answer to these criticisms of the university. Neither would relocation to the outskirts, although this would probably have been cheaper than squeezing a redeveloped campus into the given plot, with all the accompanying considerations of the city zoning plan, asbestos, concerned neighbours, and so on. Clearly the attraction of the city had to be used as an asset for the campus, and the solution was a re-visioning of the urban campus by partial redevelopment and repair.

Keeping the qualities of a traditional city campus in mind, the repair of the campus of the sixties must take into account the tension between the desire for identifiable community space, and efficiency and scale. It should fulfil the longing for a campus as a place for students and staff to be, a place that fits into the tissue of the city, provides academic identity and functionality and at the same time is financially viable. It should offer seclusion from the distractions of the city as well as being part of it.

The success of this idea depends on the degree of integration of the campus with its surroundings. Campuses not only benefit from facilities in the local neighbourhood but increase the economic support for these facilities. True integration requires high-quality public space, where the design and inhabitation of the buildings at street level is key. Walkability, and invitations to linger, reflect, meet and share knowledge, demand a rich variety of planting, with busier areas alternating with quiet places such as courtyards. People should be encouraged out of the buildings and into the streets – internal and external – to make it more like the city and less like a business district. All of this academic-urban diversity, however, requires considerable management, and has to be carefully balanced against the pressing space needs of the resident faculties.

Having established these design principles, Allford Hall Monaghan Morris (AHMM) was appointed as our architect. AHMM showed respect for Gawronski's heritage, but was courageous enough to make the bold interventions we wanted, like opening up the campus by revealing views along the canal from Roeterseiland into the surrounding neighbourhood. The endless, monotone corridors of the horizontal sixties layout have been given more variation in their dimensions, light and colour. The abundant unassigned space, fit for chance encounters, can be flexibly filled according to future needs although unclear cost allocation between departments has prevented some of the furnishing and appropriation of these spaces. Readability and wayfinding have been improved, and the academic departments and study places are now legible, offering sufficient variation to serve different users: busy and quiet, open and private. Roeterseiland has become a most vibrant place and a true part of the city, where students and employees build on a new common tradition.

Salomé A. Bentinck is a consultant and a researcher into campus and urban planning, and commissioned the remodelling of the Roeterseiland campus at UvA.

THE TREACHERY OF IMAGES

SIMON ALLFORD

Recently, on a tour of the building, and a year after the opening of the project, I was asked by a visiting critic if I could explain exactly what we had done. He was clearly somewhat baffled, circumspect even. And for different reasons I was equally circumspect of his question. For I had already explained what was old and what was new, what had been kept and what had been changed. Perhaps his bafflement was because our architecture at Roeterseiland has been as much about strategy and attitude as it has been about making an object.

For the REC A and BC complex is a twenty-first century urban palimpsest, one that resists the idea of architecture as an Instagram object. It is one where the mark of its original maker – the former Amsterdam city architect Norbert Gawronski – remains evident in the mass and the frame, and where our own interventions are just as evident in the dozen strategic moves that we designed shortly after our competition win.

That is why, in my many conversations with Norbert during the twelve-year project, I always referred to the architecture as 'his'; it is also why, at the end, when he walked around the re-completed building he spoke of 'our' project.

The University of Amsterdam project is a palimpsest that very clearly explores, tests and – in use – proved our theory and practice of the architecture of 'Theatre, Stage Set and Props'.

Indeed, I said at the interview (when the competition was down to an international shortlist of six) that whatever detailed brief for occupation we might be given by the university would soon be outdated and certainly irrelevant by the time the project opened. Even if the brief was somehow vaguely recognisable during the initial occupation of the building it would be lost in use over time.

We did not see this as a problem. Instead we regarded it as an inevitability that we could use to drive our thinking and our discussion. It also fitted in with the competition's declared aspiration to choose an architect rather than a design. Of course, that is not an uncommon competition aspiration, but it was somewhat disconcerting. The tendency, as was the case for us in this competition, is to present a product with drawings, with recognisable diagrams of plans and perspectives, and with models that are identifiable as architectural form, all with the understanding that this is merely evidence of our process. But the university's desire to focus on the approach is also why we concluded with Magritte's painting *The Treachery of Images*. His object, recognisable to all as a briar pipe, has the handwritten declaration 'Ceci n'est pas une pipe'. Our message was as clear as Magritte's: this looks like architecture but is in fact just a set of ideas.

So they did not want an architecture – at least not initially – and we did not want a brief. Of course, in the end they gave us a brief (which continued to change, as this book charts, throughout the design and build phases of the project, and is continuing to change even now as they use the spaces and rethink their uses) and we gave them an architecture! Perhaps not an architecture of the kind that appeals to some critics, an instantly legible, social-media-friendly image overlaid with words of architectural subterfuge. But it's one that recognises that architecture is to be made wherever the desire to make it exists. It's an architecture that celebrates the fact that the life of a building begins once our direct involvement in it ends – and probably long before and after that, as reflected in the huge timespan (1637 to 2018 and beyond!) of this book. It's an architecture that delights in the challenge of re-expressing both the horizontality inherent in Gawronski's REC A tower and the elegant monotony of frame of his canal-spanning REC BC slab. We embraced these traces as they are a useful reminder of a skin that was once there and an inevitable expression of a frame that lies just beneath our new skin. For the same reasons we were clear that the real challenge was not to 'reposition the building': we did not want to remove the very generous frame but instead intervene to reconnect it with the city.

That is why, having fixed on a generous strategy of promenade as linear room, using the past, present and future life of the city and campus to inform the architecture around it, we pursued in construction the strategic moves that we had established as the project's underlying idea. These were to remove all the skin and much slab; to create houses as public rooms around mini atria and passage; to build new bridges across the canal and in the sky; to create an architectural promenade that connected city street to formal teaching spaces, itself housing informal study landscapes. And then we remade the building's skin to express the life behind this multi-layered city sandwich. That is why our project became both an urban and architectural one.

This strategy has generated a particular architecture – and a new set of images, more grounded in the city, less Insta-ready. The removal of a chunk of building that blocked the axial view along the canal reconnects the dying campus behind it to the living city. The new bridge at ground level over the canal is traditional in its profile – it is regulated to be thus – but in plan it becomes a stopping place as well as a crossing point. It bridges a canal whose banks – in an unfamiliar way to the traditional Amsterdam quayside – are stepped down to enjoy the water, making a new place in the city. Above, the new bridge in the sky frames the reopened city view from without and within, bringing a memorable conclusion to the students' architectural promenade. This promenade begins at the passage – a new public room through which twenty thousand students a day pass on their way to the thirteen very different lecture halls, and a myriad of smaller seminar and tutorial and teaching rooms.

The essential architectural brief was to create a building where students would come to lectures and then enjoy staying and studying, informally engaging in conversation with their peers. That the students have complained about being unable to find enough free study landscape spaces and that the amount of bike parking will need to double (taking an opportunity identified during the design phases) is evidence that the urban architecture of Theatre, Stage Set and Props* is working – and may indeed be a victim of its own success. The campus has become a piece of city where public and students intermingle: it's identifiable simultaneously as both a university and a piece of Amsterdam.

To survive into the future the lasting image of this reinvented piece of city will be key: in the long term no-one will keep a building that does not have a memorable presence. From the outset we were clear that if the project was to successfully survive future adaptation it should have a clear and robust identity that would enable it, even during construction, to accommodate the work of others. That is why we were engaged in the setting-up of competitions that resulted in the appointment of the graphic designers Hat Trick, the artist Barbara Broekman, and landscape designers Inside Outside, as well as a host of architects appointed to do anything from a room within 'our' architecture to a building within the site, behind the barrier-building that our interventions had re-connected.

The pictures tell of the import of this architectural story to us as authors. The strategies of horizontal and vertical, shadow and recess, matt and gloss, black and white, and a scaling up from windows and mini-atria to the canal-spanning, hanging glass room of the bridge, create a richly detailed and highly specific architecture of megastructure.

The unimaginatively named REC ABC project (the naming rights was one briefing that we lost) is about the creation of an architecture that believes in the resilience and delight, which starts with an attitude towards movement and time, and finishes with a simple and legible object. As the critic Jospeh Rykwert noted, "To have restructured a university campus to everybody's satisfaction is almost suspicious. The architects of any existing structure are usually defensive of their achievement; academics — a doggedly conservative lot — tend to be very attached to their existing quarters, however cramped and awkward they may have been; and students are always a fractious though inevitably a fluctuating group (and in Amsterdam they have been particularly restless in recent years). To have won the assent, even the approval of these three constituencies – as AHMM seems to have done – is already a vast, if a subjective achievement. It all seems to fit together as if it had been devised as such from the outset. When you visit the buildings, you would never suspect that its making was such a tortuous and awkward process. It feels very much as if it had resulted from a sequence of straightforward and simple decisions."

Which to me perfectly answers the question posed by the visiting critic as to what we've actually done at Roeterseiland. Now we have finished our work, the life of the building has begun. UvA looks like architecture, but not the architecture of Instagram. UvA is the architecture of the city overlaid into a found frame, an appropriate and delightful idea of architecture in promenade and on palimpsest, a theatre for everyday life.

*The theatre is a setting for everyday life, an object in the city that should last for a hundred years and beyond. It is subject to forces of change that are acknowledged by stage sets, buildings within a building that accommodate specific needs and that may last for up to twenty years. These resolve the tension between the generics of the city and the specific needs of the user. The changing needs of everyday life are then addressed by props, architectural furniture that allows universal space to be reconfigured. It is this tripartite arrangement that allows a building to be both endlessly reconfigurable and architecturally memorable.

Simon Allford is a founder of Allford Hall Monaghan Morris, and led the architectural team rethinking the Roeterseiland campus.

PHASE -1

1637–2007

IN WHICH A CITY – AND A UNIVERSITY – GROW, MASTERPLANS ARE MADE AND A COMPETITION IS WON

Small-scale industrial premises at Roeterseiland in around 1930 (top); Norbert Gawronski (bottom)

The medieval centre of Amsterdam was, until the late sixteenth century, protected at its outer edge by the Singel, a fortified moat. As the city expanded, further concentric rings of canals were built to encircle the old medieval port and town. They were contained within the Singelgracht, dug in 1872 for defence and water management, which today still marks the edge of the historic centre.

During the eighteenth century the western canals had become lined with tall, gabled houses and monuments that expressed Amsterdam's trading wealth, while those in the east remained more industrial in character, with small workshops and warehouses clustered along their banks. At Roeterseiland, home of the University of Amsterdam's main inner-city campus, this industrial use continued right up until the early part of the twentieth century, and the urban character of the area was further cemented with the building of Sarphatistraat, the inner-city ring road, along the southern edge of the university site.

The University of Amsterdam (UvA) traces its roots back to 1632, the city's Golden Age. Building on its trading wealth, Amsterdam wanted its young people to develop a wide outlook on the world and to be active in international business. The university – then known as the Athenaeum Illustre (Illustrious School) – operated out of converted buildings in the city centre, as well as the headquarters of the Dutch East India Company. Many of these buildings are still occupied by the UvA, but as the university grew during the nineteenth and twentieth centuries and began to need larger facilities, bespoke buildings were built further away from the city centre, first in the Plantagebuurt and later across the Muidergracht on Roeterseiland.

After the second world war, the university expanded rapidly, and a masterplan was drawn up by city architect Norbert Gawronski to extend the UvA campus at Roeterseiland. Gawronski was born in Poland in 1925, and escaped internment by the German occupying forces during the second world war by fleeing to France, where he joined the Free Polish Army. After the war he completed his architectural training in London, before settling with his Dutch wife, Emmy, in the Netherlands. There he became an architect for Amsterdam's Public Works Department.

His masterplan for Roeterseiland, sitting in the south-eastern corner of the Singelgracht, had as its core idea a long, L-shaped slab block spanning over the Nieuwe Achtergracht to connect the north and south islands, with a pair of gateway point towers to the west on either side of the canal's intersection with Roetersstraat. The buildings would be linked at first-floor level by a system of pedestrian walkways and terraces, reached by grand stairs rising from open piazzas at street level.

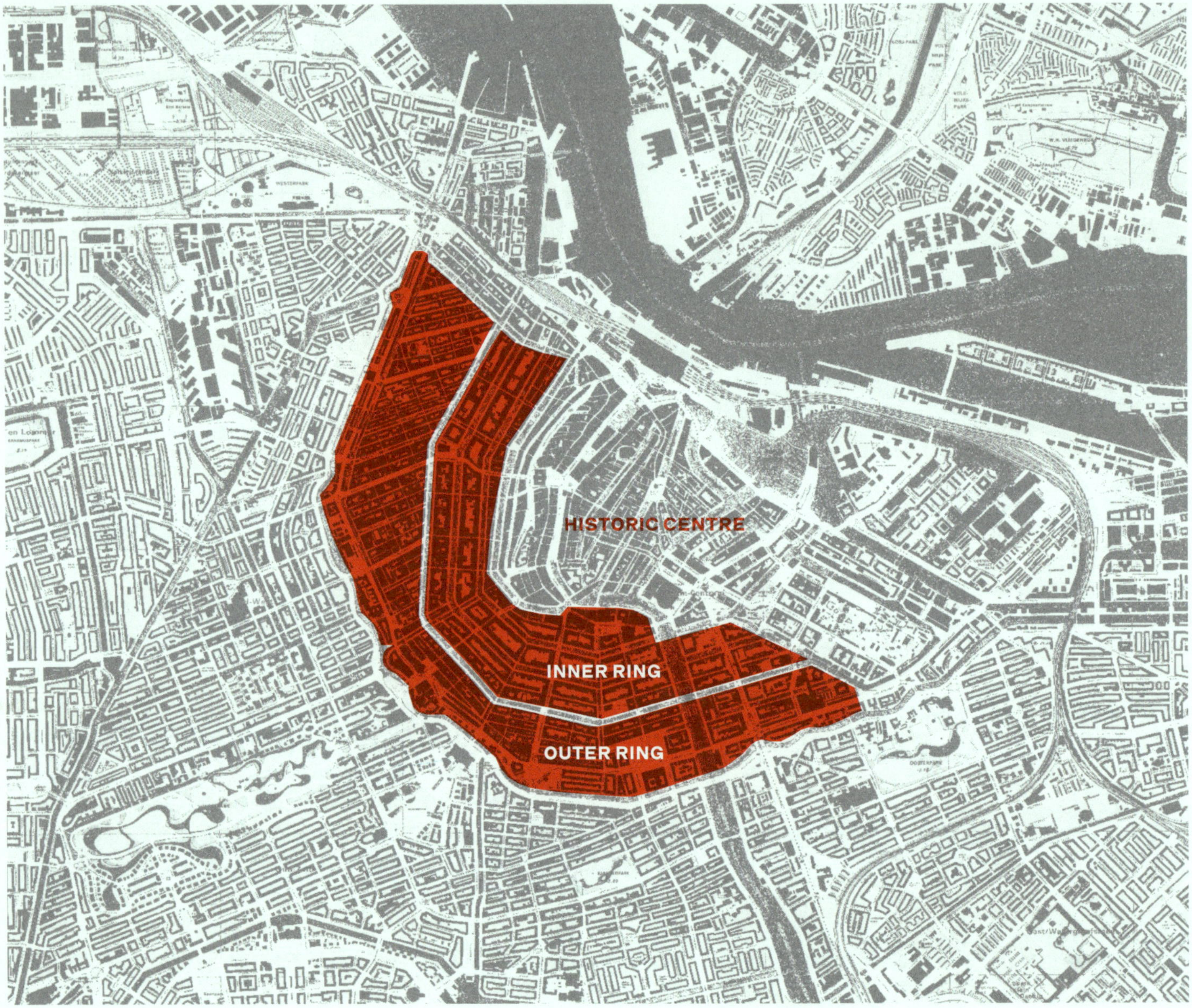

The city story: canal-building around the historic centre, in four concentric rings, began during the seventeenth century. There were two main phases of development – the area to the north-west of the Leidsegracht was completed first, and that to the south-east by around 1700. During the nineteenth century an outer ring of development with a more radial layout of canals was completed within the newly dug Singelgracht.

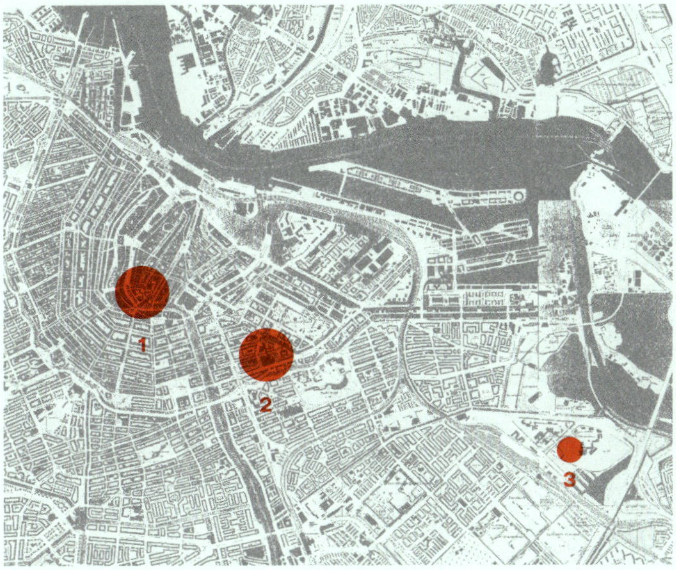

2005

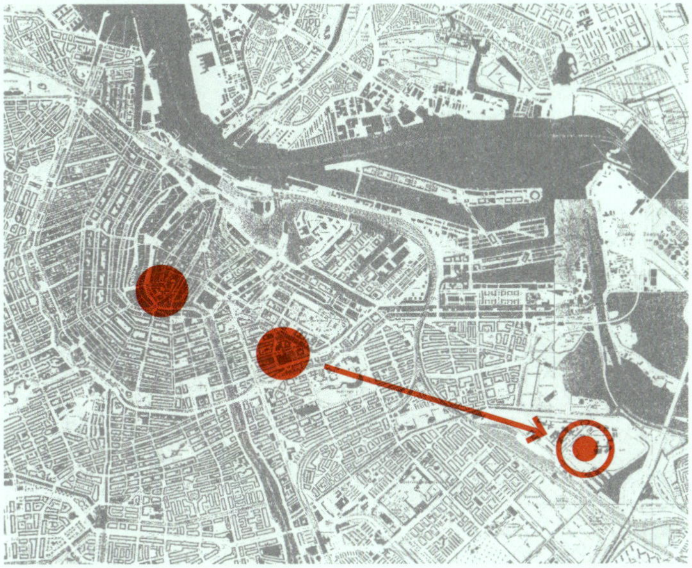

by 2012

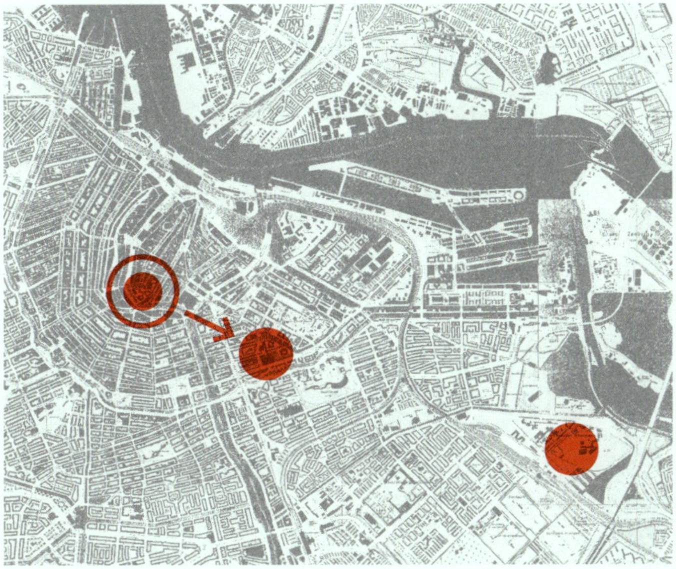

by 2017

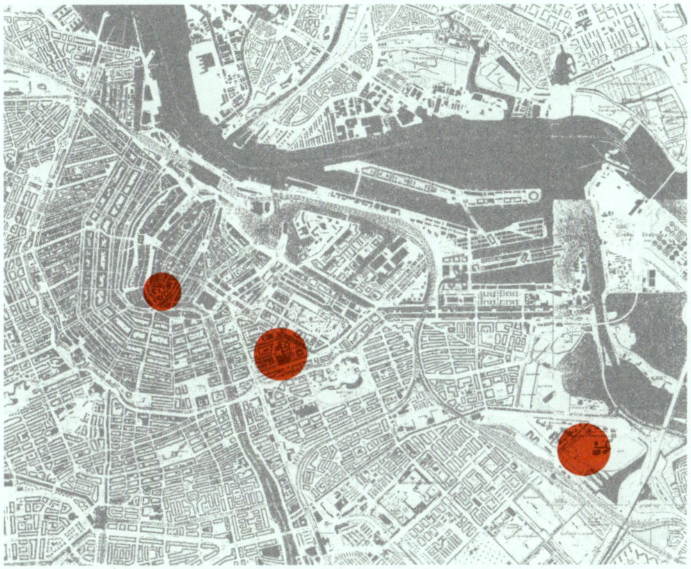

2018

1 City centre
2 Roeterseiland
3 Science Park

The university story: the consolidation of the UvA's estate in Amsterdam has brought about a general shift of students from the historic centre to new, extended campuses at Roeterseiland and the Science Park to the east of the city.

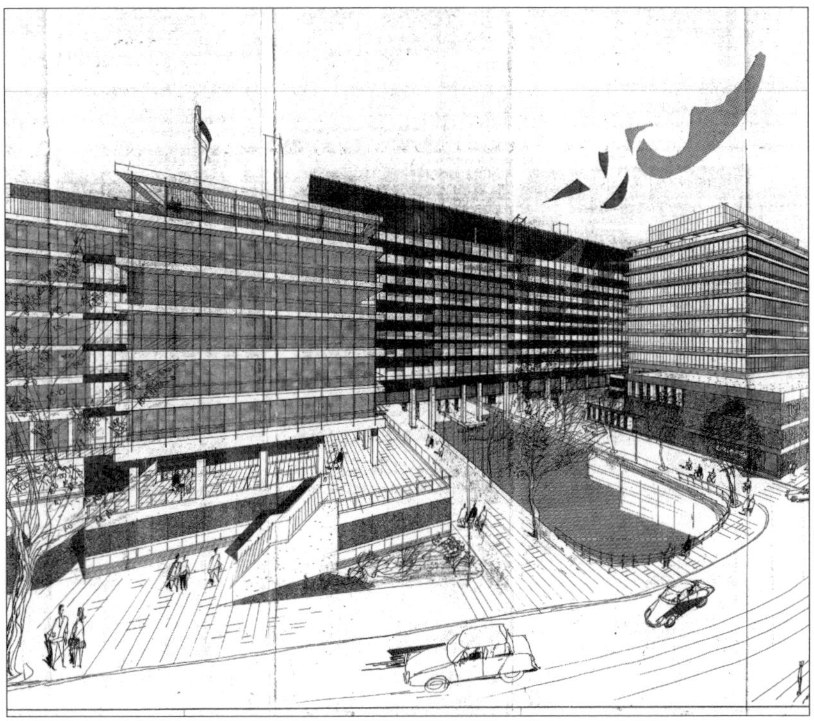

Perspectives and isonometric drawing of Gawronski's campus at Roeterseiland.

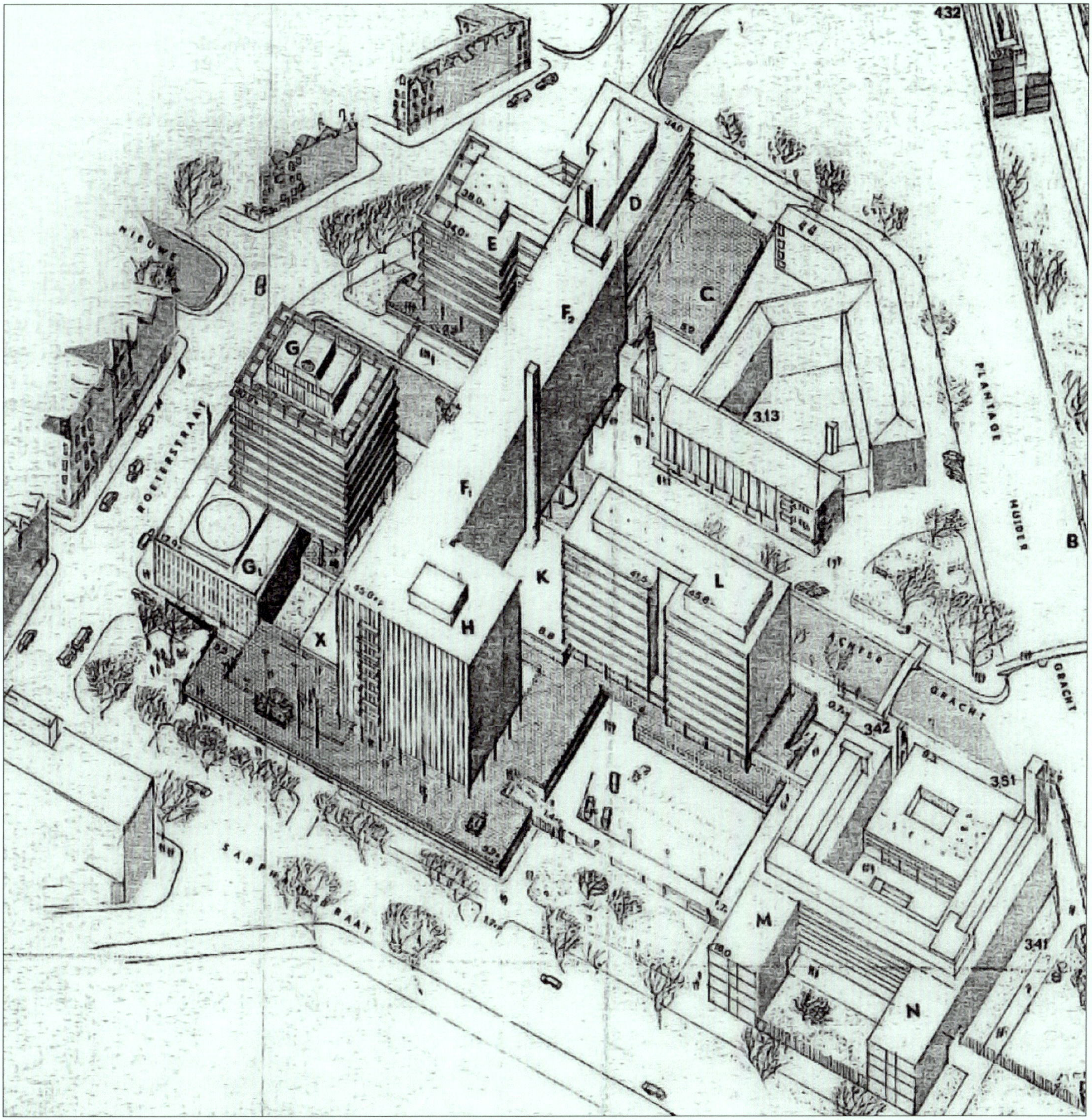

NIEUWE
ROETERSSTRAAT
SARPHATISTRAAT
PLANTAGE
MUIDER
ACHTER
GRACHT
GRACHT
A
B
C
D
E
F₂
F₁
G
G₁
H
K
L
M
N
X
4,32
3,13
3,42
3,51
3,41

The Roeterseiland campus in 2000 (right).

The unrealised raised pedestrian access level left views along the canal blocked (top), and uncomfortable connections into the building from the canalside (bottom).

Ultimately, only part of Gawronski's scheme was realised: a single point block, today known as REC A (from Building A, Roeterseiland Complex), and the canal-spanning block, built in two stages and as a result now known as REC BC. Lecture theatres were contained within the tower podium and underground parking was provided.

Gawronski's realised buildings were by far the largest on the Roeterseiland campus, and typical of functional modernist design. REC BC was a 136-metre-long slab with a reinforced concrete frame and a curtain wall of horizontal strip windows. The REC A tower rose from a solid podium, with the floor-to-soffit glazing system recessed back to leave a stack of projecting floor slabs as the primary architectural feature. Elsewhere on Roeterseiland, the university occupied and redeveloped sites on an ad-hoc basis: several of the older brick warehouses and buildings of the Amsterdam School were refurbished for teaching and social uses, while other new-build additions had more expressive forms and massing.

Today, UvA has more than 5,000 staff teaching over 30,000 students across seven faculties. During the early 2000s, it became clear that its disparate property holdings had to be updated, and that they needed to be less spread out: many faculties were working out of several locations. As a result, the university decided to consolidate its accommodation into a series of 'hubs' across the city, each with its own distinct academic character.

The largest, and most contained, campus would be at Roeterseiland, home to the Faculties of Economics and Business, Social and Behavioural Sciences, and Law. This campus would also become the cultural heart of the university, with the relocation here of CREA – a centre offering arts courses, performances and student support.

However, Gawronski's partly realised vision for Roeterseiland presented some conflicts. The REC BC slab block divided the campus in two and was perceived as a barrier. Its low opening over the canal, designed to reflect the original raised pedestrian access level, created an unwelcoming underpass on the towpath and blocked the linear canal views for which the city is famous. Alongside the canal, the podium of REC A accommodated useful lecture theatres, but presented a blank external face.

On the other hand, these large and robust buildings, located on a valuable and central waterside site, presented a great opportunity to redefine Roeterseiland as an open city campus. In 2004, UvA commissioned a masterplan by Palmboom + van den Bout (now Palmbout Urban Landscapes), with the aim of revitalising the campus through new construction and refurbishment. There was an emphasis on repairing the streetscape, bringing the canal to life as the principal axis of the campus,

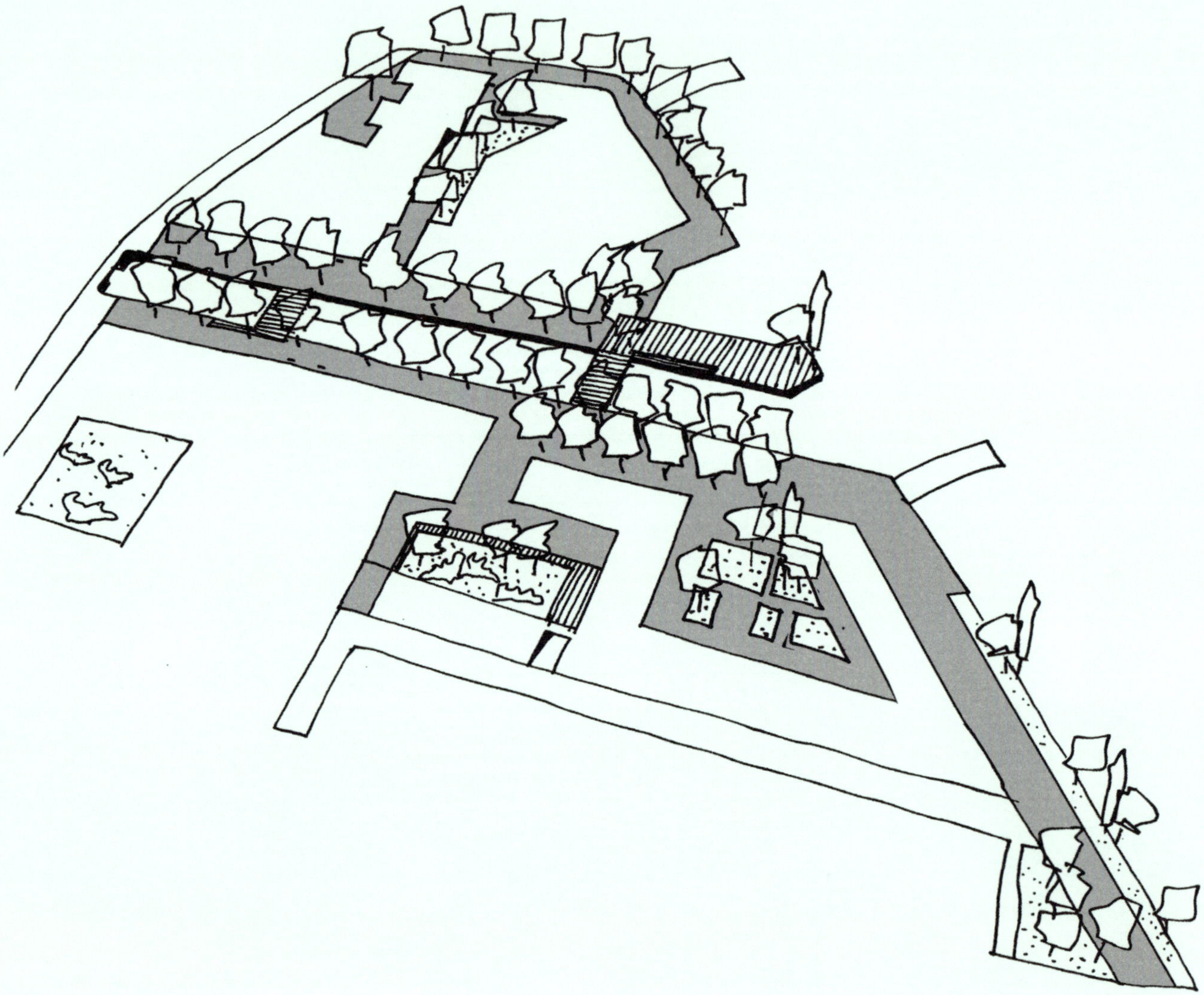

Like Magritte's famous pipe, AHMM's competition approach was to overlay an existing scenario with a fresh interpretation. In this case, the team took the Palmbout masterplan (left) and, rather than designing specific buildings within it and relying on the 'treachery of images', developed a broader idea of what the campus might become.

Competition drawing, envisaging a well-connected campus focused around the canal. (overleaf)

a living spine onto which the adjoining buildings would open. Once the Palmbout masterplan was complete, an international ideas competition was launched for the reconfiguration of the largest of the buildings on Roeterseiland: Gawronski's legacy of slab and point blocks and podiums.

AHMM's proposals investigated how the complex could better be connected to the city. Gawronski's original scheme had made the site permeable by way of high-level pedestrian walkways. With the primary access not at street level, and a renewed focus on the canalside areas, a new secondary axis was suggested, running through the campus along the length of the slab block. This new thoroughfare could be reinforced with a bridge across the canal, and driven further south by introducing a passage between RECs A and BC. The existing structures would be recycled, but a large opening would be created in the slab block to lighten the dark, compressed space over the canal and to reveal longer views.

The reshaped interiors would serve a new mix of functions and occupants, making the most of the flexibility offered by the existing structure. Accessible rooftops would be introduced to take full advantage of the height of the buildings, creating high-level 'living rooms'. The facades would be renewed to improve environmental comfort for occupants, to aid orientation from within, and to establish Roeterseiland's identity within the city.

AHMM was appointed to the project in spring 2007, by which time the university had already adopted the idea of introducing a secondary axis to the masterplan, regarding it as fundamental to realising their aspiration for the 'City as Campus'.

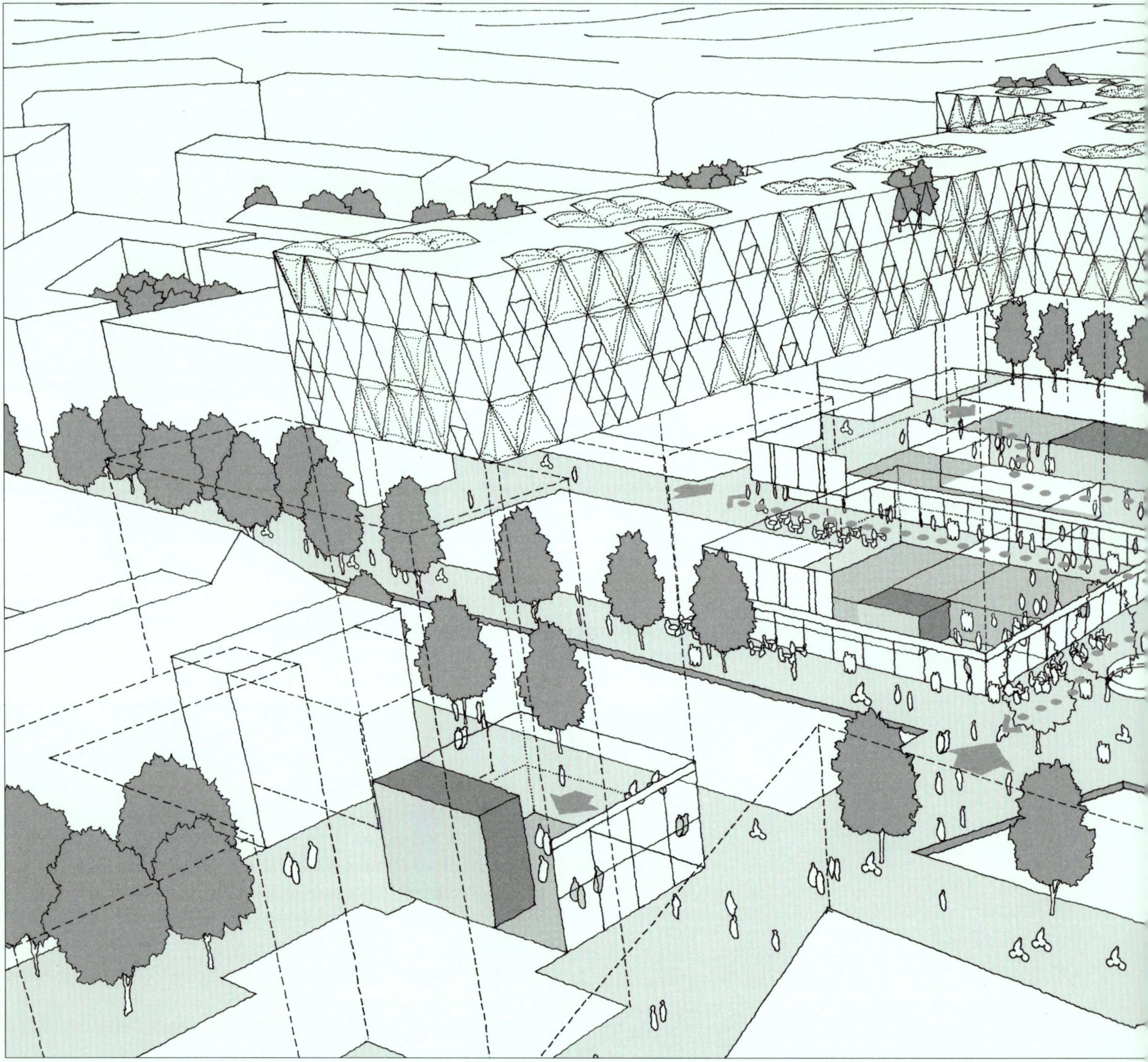

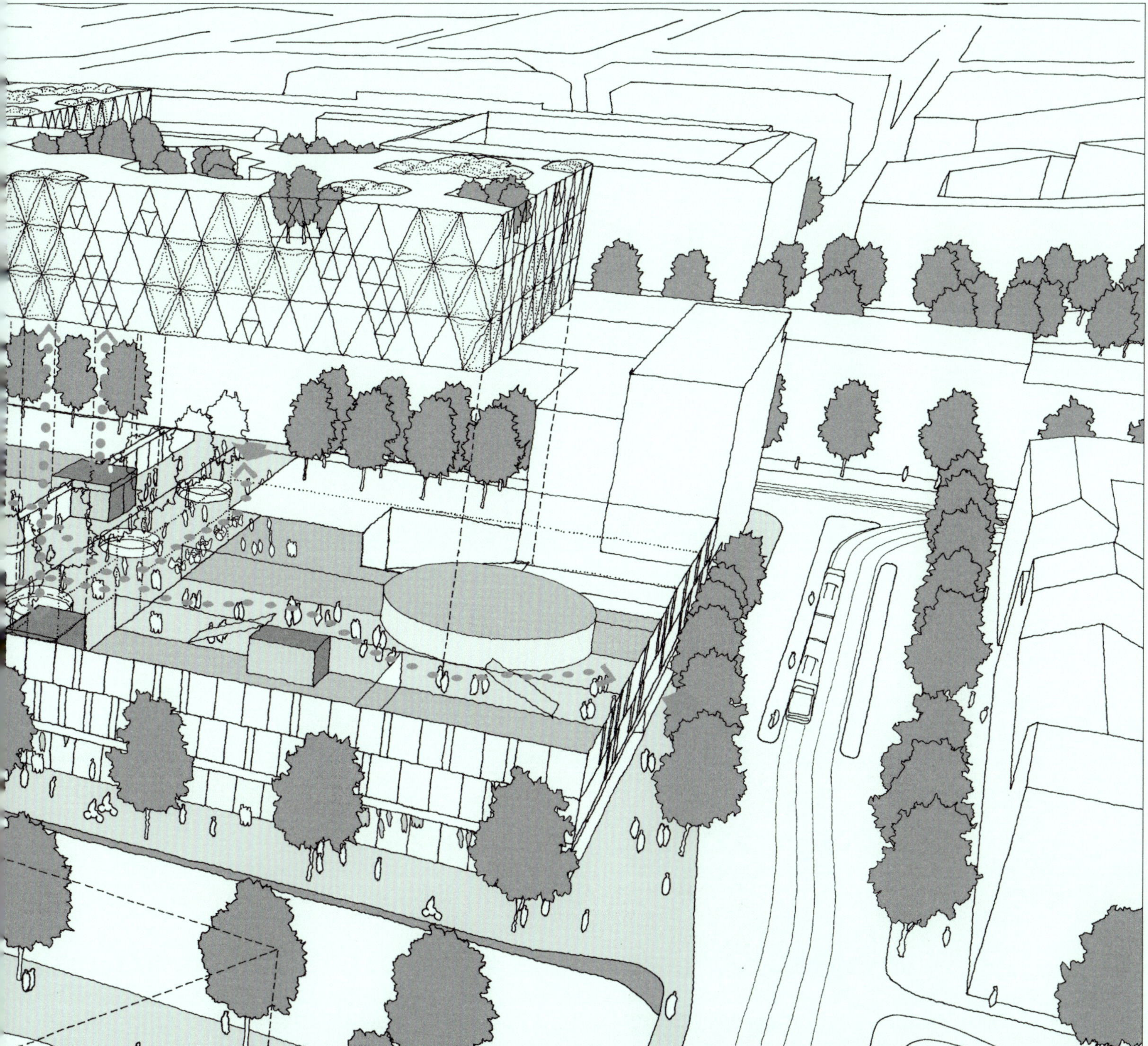

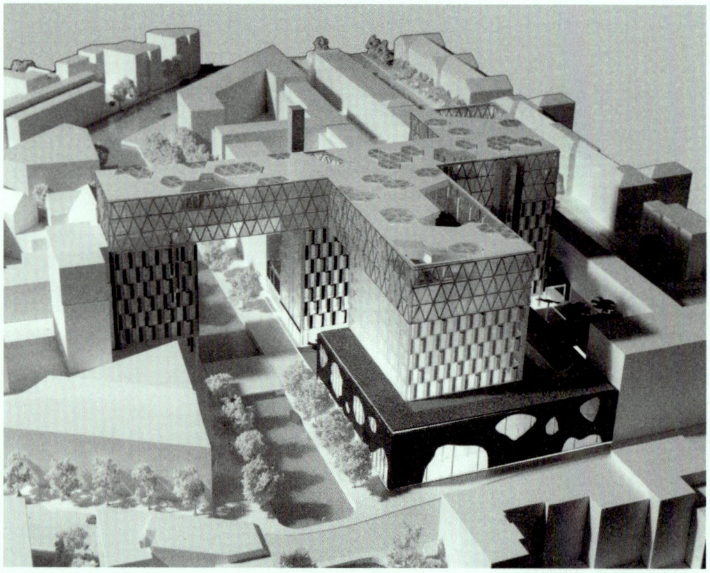

PHASE 0

JUN–SEP 07

IN WHICH A UNIVERSITY'S FUTURE IS CONDENSED INTO FOUR A4 PAGES AND A SERIES OF STRATEGIC MOVES

Surprisingly for a project of this ambition, the concept brief was summarised in just four A4 pages – although the university were clear that the detailed brief would continue to evolve as the building's key user groups negotiated their space needs. The decision-making process was complex, involving the university departments responsible for procuring and delivering new facilities, as well as the academic faculties that would be based within them.

HUISVESTINGSONTWIKKELING

Memo 25 May 2007
to : AHMM
via : Salomé Bentinck, Piet Zwinkels
from : Ton Boon
topic : Basic Programme of Requirements buildings REC ABC

For the redevelopment of the buildings REC ABC a programme of requirements is being made. The architect has been selected and has to start the structure study while the exact programme is not yet finished. This memo will give the requirements for this structure study.

Programme of requirements REC ABC

The programme of requirements for buildings REC A/B/C exists of the following outlines:

- A minimum of 8.600 m2 net floor area (nfa) educational facilities, consisting of :
    - 1.500 m2 large lecture halls (appr.1.200 seats in total)
    - 5.200 m2 small workgroup rooms (appr. 2.600 seats), a minimum of 15p a room, to be linked to other rooms to place 30p, 45p and 60p, the exact assortment will be decided on later.
    - 1.900 m2 study places (appr. 720 seats)
- 4.000 m2 nfa flexible space suitable for both offices and workgroup rooms.
- A minimum of 16.900 m2 nfa office workplaces, meeting facilities and storage space.
- 2.200 m2 nfa specific lab facilities (for Psychology, exact specifications will be given later on)
- 1.500 m2 nfa sports facilities (1 fitness hall, 4 multifunctional halls, dressing rooms)
- 1.500 m2 nfa for the student information centre (reception functions, room for folders etc, several PC workplaces and office workplaces for employees)
- 1.500 – 2.000 m2 catering facilities

The total programme consists of appr. **36.200 m^2 net floor area.**

Besides that there also has to be made a:

- covered cycle storage for appr. 2.000 bicycles in the basement
- as many as possible car and motorcycle parking spaces in the basement.

Planning REC A/B/C

The planning outlines for the redevelopment of REC A/B/C are defined in the document "Overall Planning REC ABC" d.d. 01/06/07 by Royal Haskoning. The major milestones for the design fase are:

- Structure study ready August 2007
- Preliminary design ready December 2007
- Final design August 2008

Budget

The budget for REC ABC has been set on € 32.000.000 for buildings costs, €15.000.000,- for building services and € 2.000.000,- for fitting-out . This was based on the original size of the buildings of 56.000 m2 gross floor area. We found that the exact size of the buildings is bigger than that (appr. 68.000 m2 gross floor area).

For the structure study the starting principle is the budget per square meter. This is €571/m2 for building costs, € 268/m2 for building services and € 36/m2 for fitting-out. After finishing the structure study the exact budget will be determined.

ECM \ g:\ahmm jobs 2006\06042 university of amsterdam\1.00 client\1.10 client briefing\received\2007\070618_basicpor_p0\070618_13.10mn016 basic por rec abc 070525.doc 2 - pag. van 4

Urban plan

The design has to fit in the zoning plan of the municipality and the urban plan which has been made by Palmboom & van den Bout. The following outlines are important to adopt in the design for buildings REC ABC:

- The Nieuwe Achtergracht is the new central open space in which all entrances should be placed;
- The lecture halls should be clustered and placed on the lower levels of the building, near to the main entrances. The counter facilities (student info) and study places should be placed around these halls and along main passageways (see figure);
- The buildings will be separated to encourage the visitors to use the public space on the ground level;
- The design has to be open plan and transparent on the ground floor in relation to the outside public space;
- The ground level has to be transparent and filled with lively functions which have a clear relation to the outside space;
- If possible keep the large lecture halls in place (REC A), because of costs and construction;
- The buildings have to be suitable for multifunctional use in regards of structure, dimensions and building services;
- Keep the existing concrete casco (incl. elevators and stairs) and the existing building volumes (zoning plan);
- Remove the lowest floor of building C, above the Nieuwe Achtergracht;
- The construction of two new entrances at the Nieuwe Achtergracht and one at the Sarphatistraat as in the urban plan;
- Replacement of the facades, the building services and the fitting-out. If possible keep part of the existing fitting-out, for example the large lecture hall in building A, to reduce costs;
- Clear routing for large groups of students in the buildings;

ECM \ g:\ahmm jobs 2006\06042 university of amsterdam\1.00 client\1.10 client briefing\received\2007\070618_basicpor_p0\070618_13.10mn016 basic por rec abc 070525.doc 3 - pag. van 4

- Redesign the parking space in relation to a clear routing and new entrance and exit;

Spatial development model buildings ABC

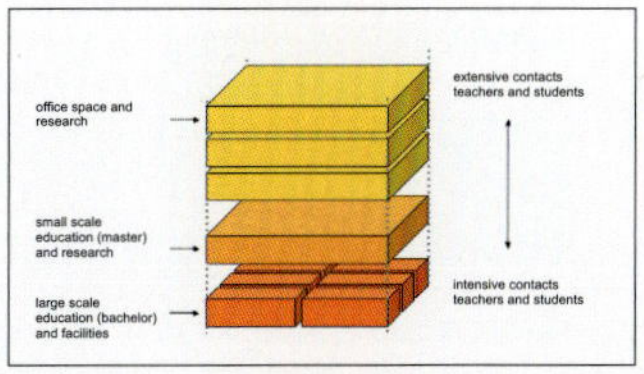

ECM \ g:\ahmm jobs 2006\06042 university of amsterdam\1.00 client\1.10 client briefing\received\2007\070618_basicpor_p0\070618_13.10mn016 basic por rec abc 070525.doc 4 - pag. van 4

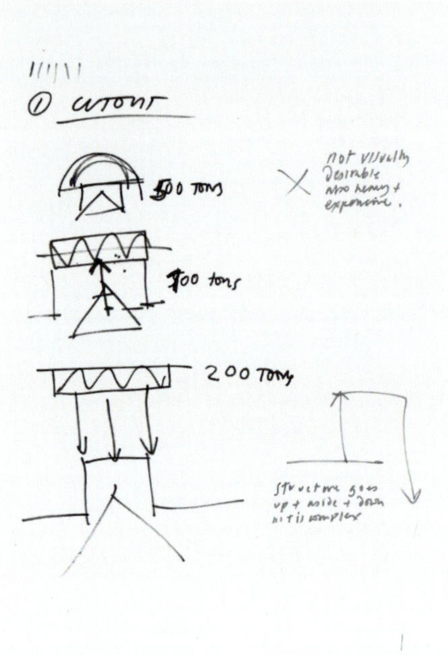

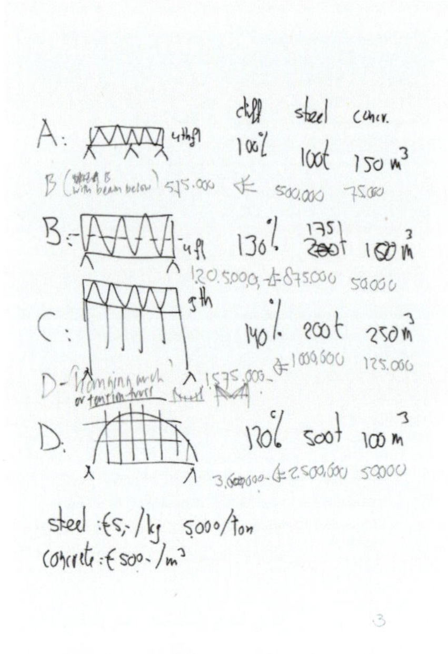

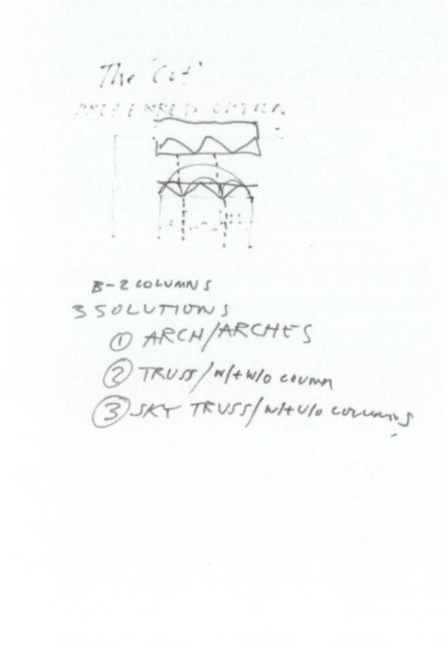

The project was structured around a series of strategic moves, refined from the ideas proposed in the competition. These included the facade improvements, the cut through the main slab block, a bridge across the canal, the introduction of the connecting passage, the opening up of mini atria inside the slab and the expression of departmental houses, and the insertion of larger spaces such as public rooms and lecture rooms.

Strategy workshops with the client began by looking at the cut, and specifically the dimensions of the new aperture in the slab block. How big would it need to be to frame new views down the canal? And of what proportions? A series of studies would establish an appropriate scale for the opening, balanced against the technique, risks and costs associated with realising it.

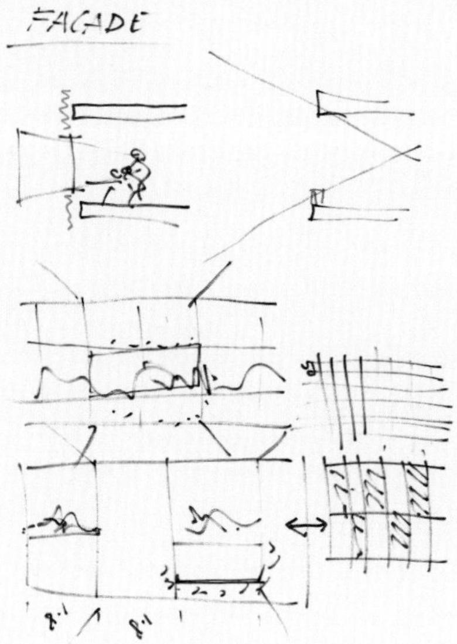

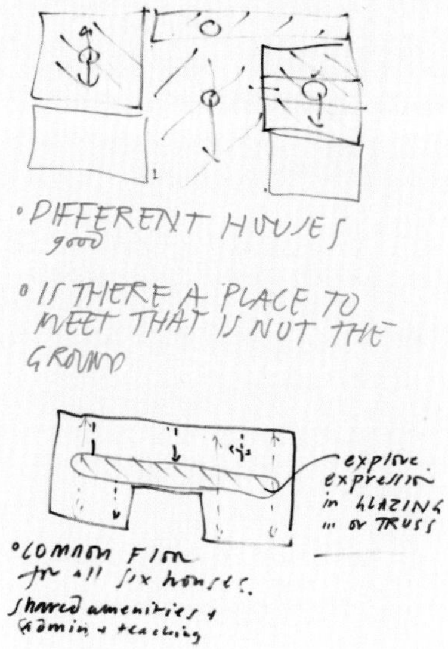

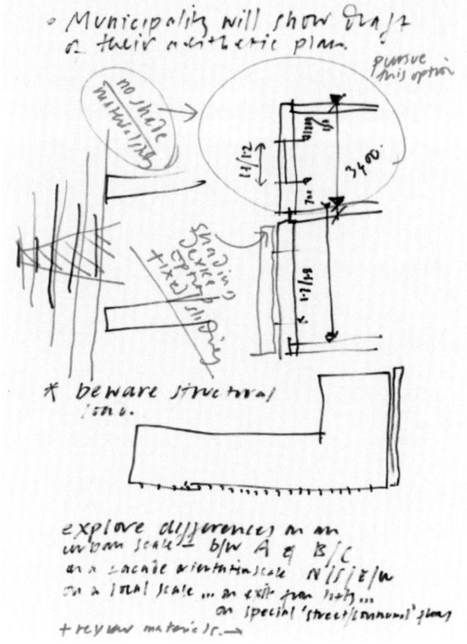

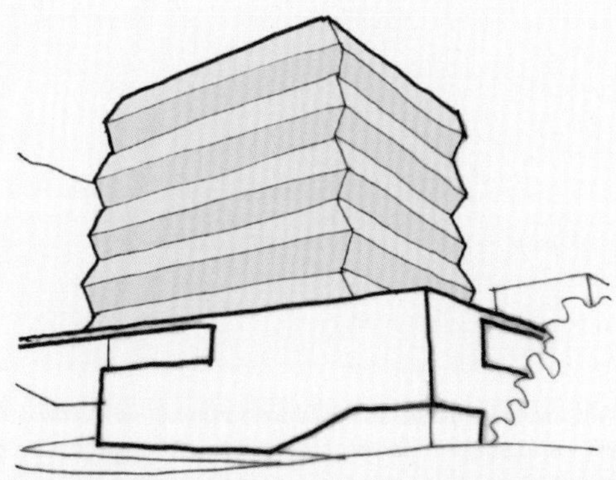

Early workshops also looked at how the existing buildings might be articulated in the city, and how different facade treatments could make them work visually as an ensemble of related, yet complementary, volumes.

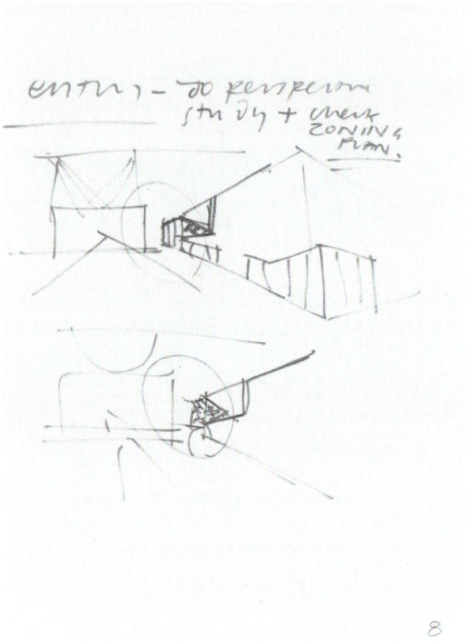

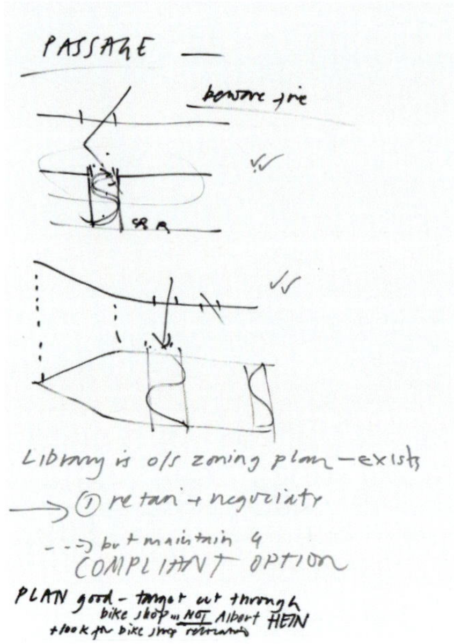

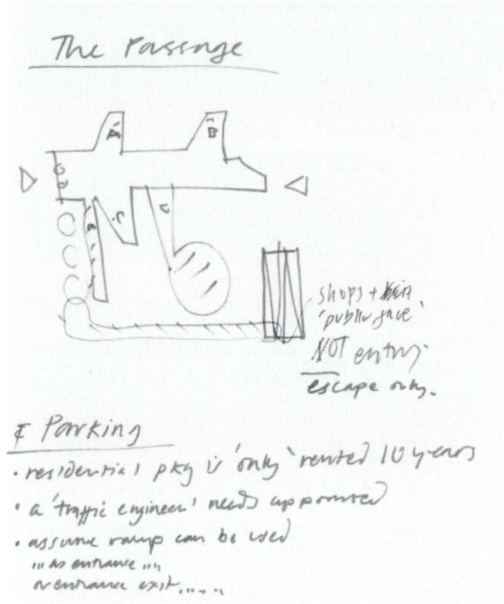

How should the entrance to the new passage between the two blocks be articulated – and scaled? Externally its scale needed to sit with that of the new canal bridge, marking the address, drawing in both pedestrians and cyclists, and guiding them towards their destination.

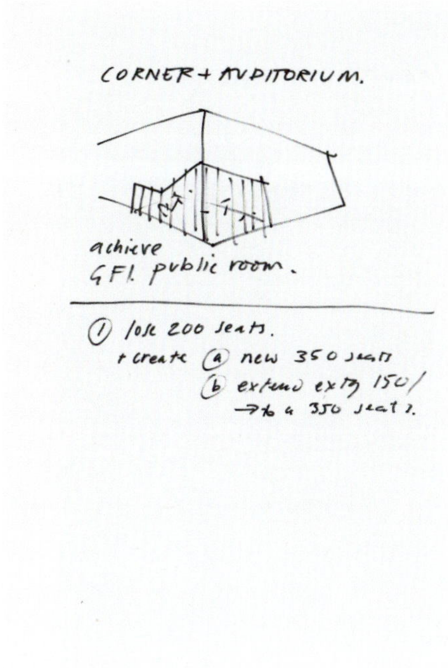

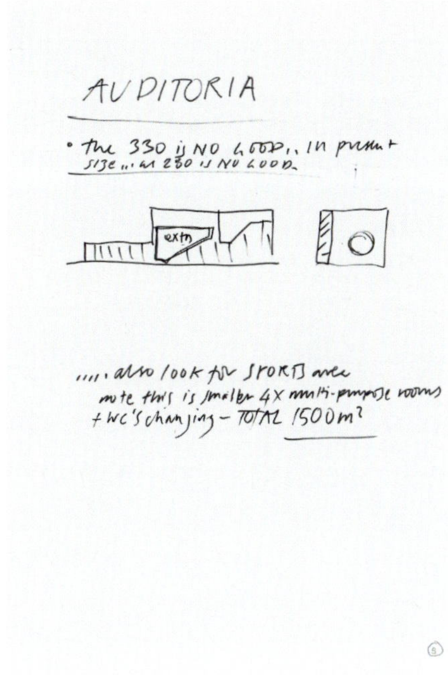

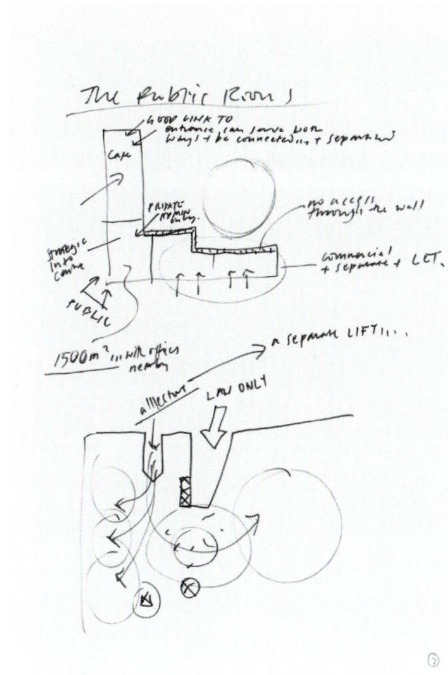

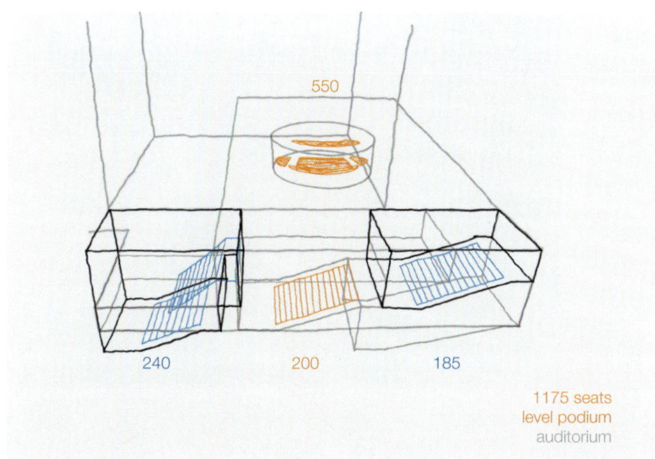

The strategic workshops also marked the infancy of a lecture-room brief. The university needed a suite of auditoria and lecture rooms to be shared between faculties, and various configurations within the podium were tested.

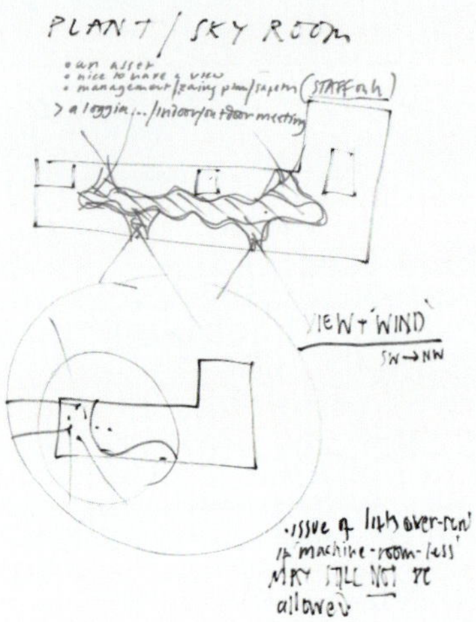

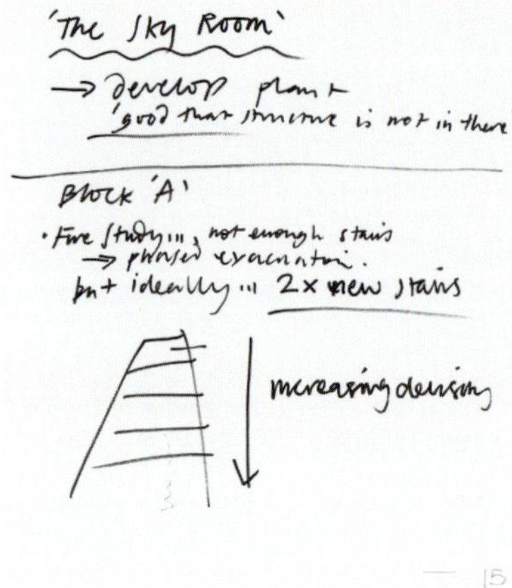

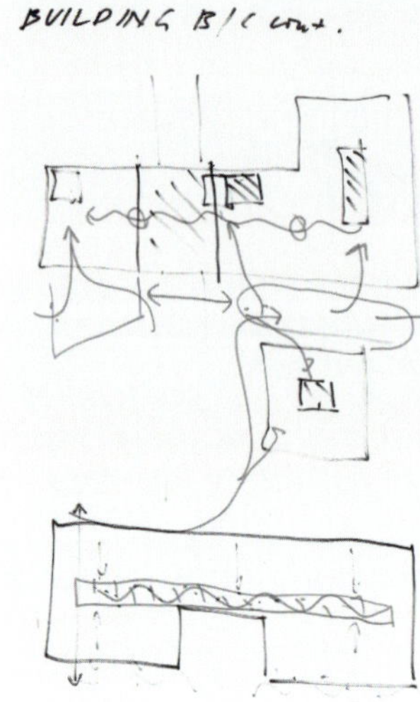

Competition proposals for a sky room enjoying views across Amsterdam were tested against the city zoning plan (Bestemmingsplan), which sets out the massing and use for all buildings. It was not permitted: the historic city of Amsterdam was not to have any megastructure larger than that existing. However, plans for a city room with views within the existing mass continued to evolve.

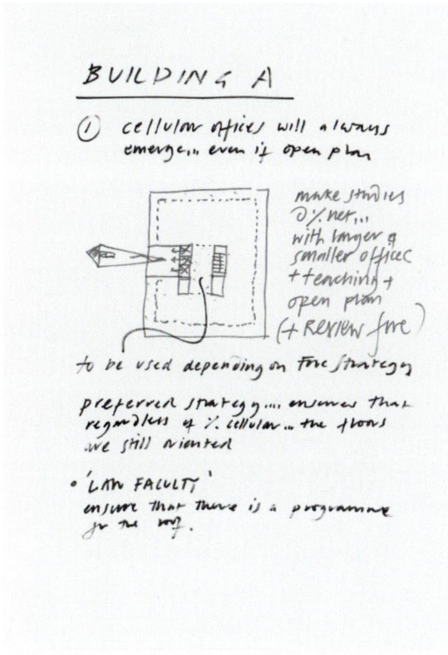

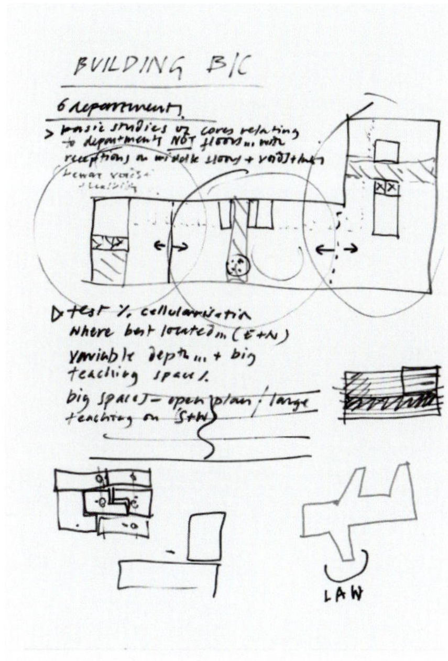

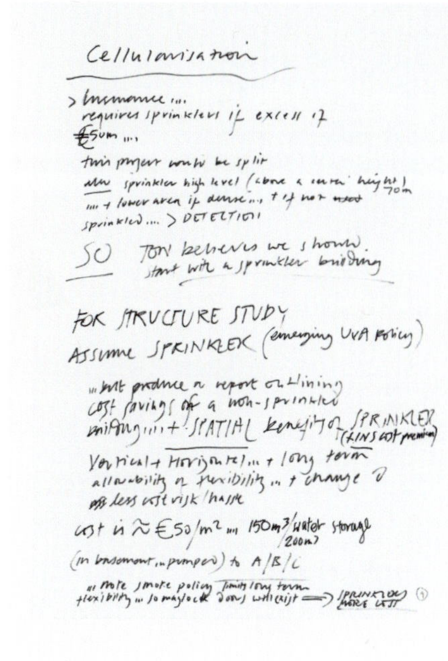

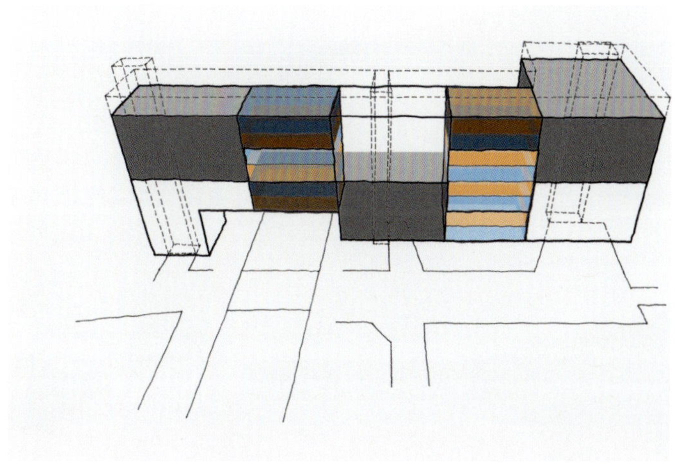

Early strategies were sketched out for the arrangement of teaching and academic office space in the slab block. Swing zones between each circulation core could expand or contract according to the space needs of each department over time.

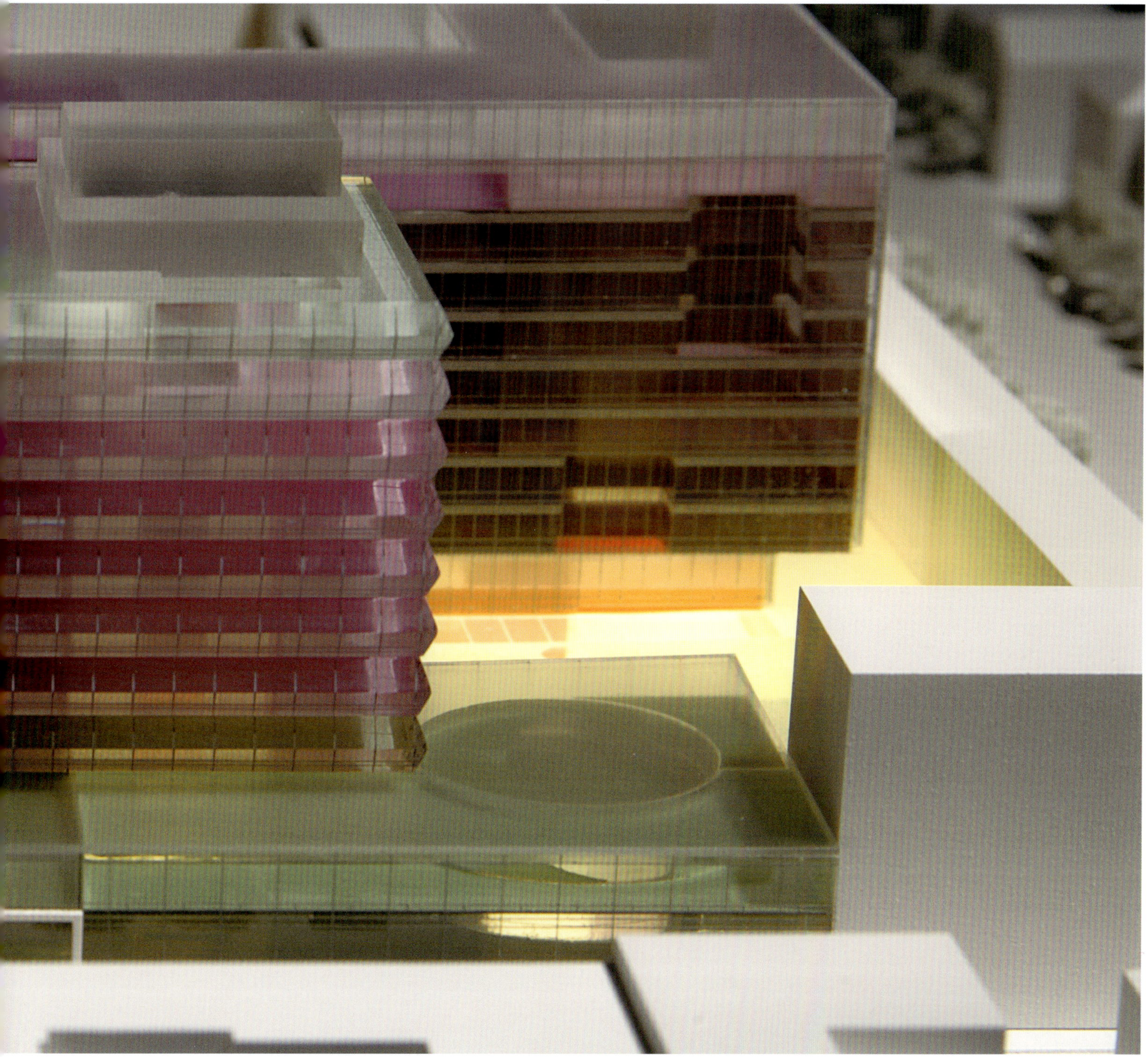

Conceptual models helped to describe the developing design strategy to a multitude of stakeholders.

PHASE 1

SEP 07–MAR 08

IN WHICH WE ENGINEER A CUT, STUDY BRIDGE GEOMETRY AND START A PROMENADE

A visual survey of Amsterdam canal bridges revealed some common features: they have clear spans to avoid obstructing the water flow and minimal headroom for passing boats, meaning the approach roads do not have to rise too high to cross them.

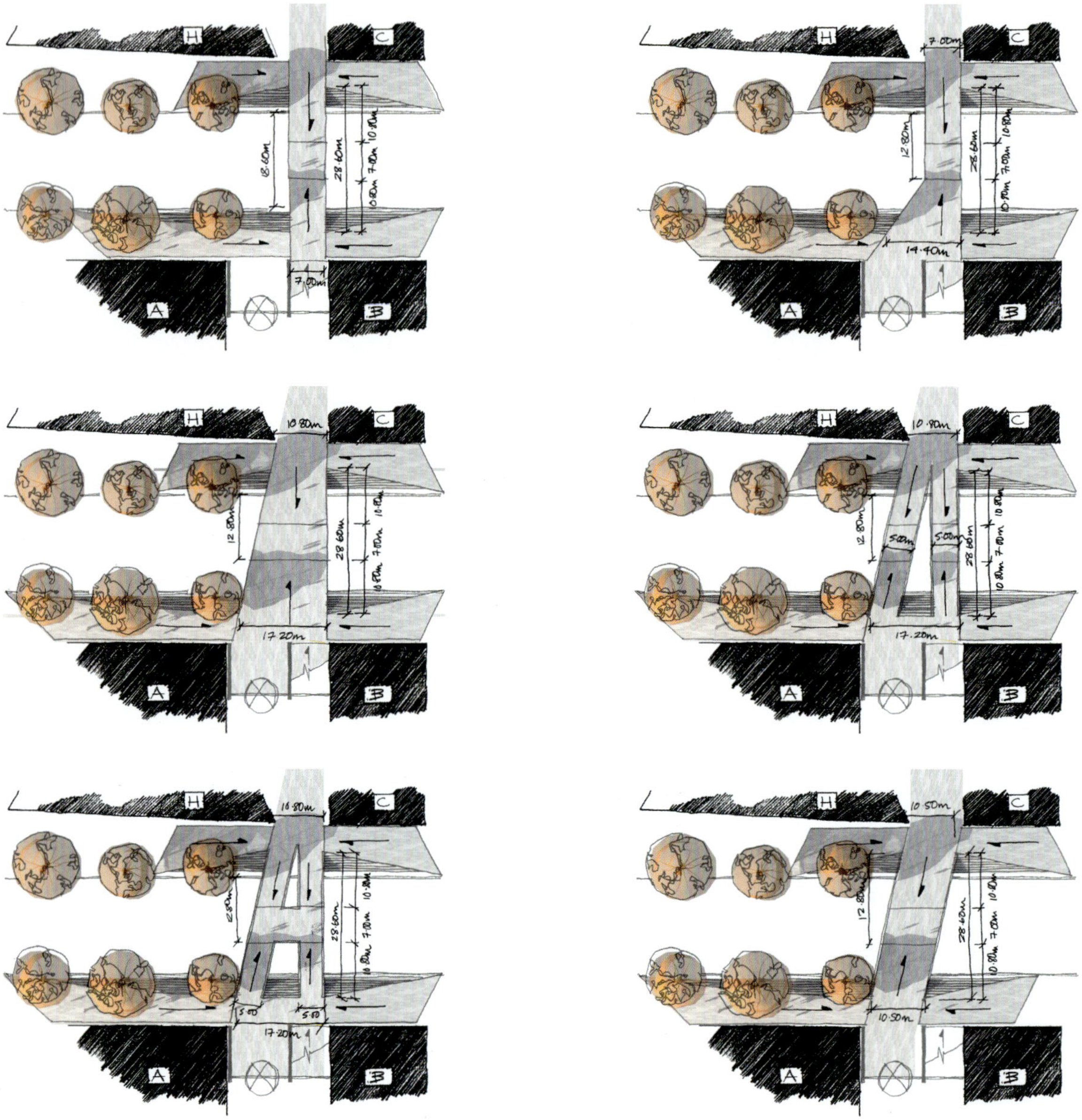

The bridge across Nieuwe Achtergracht on the secondary axis across campus needed to effectively become a piece of urban landscape, aligning with the varying geometry of the buildings at either end and flowing into the existing canalside routes.

Moving off the bridge and into the passage, the experience of the user was critical: how would students navigate around a building of this scale? Journeys through the building were visualised, with models developed to show how these promenades would work across interconnected spaces at multiple levels.

The complex spaces within the passage itself were also visualised in a 3D model (1). Vertical circulation was added (2) along with structural elements (3). Enclosing walls were added (4), before the different levels of the space were studied in more detail (5, 6).

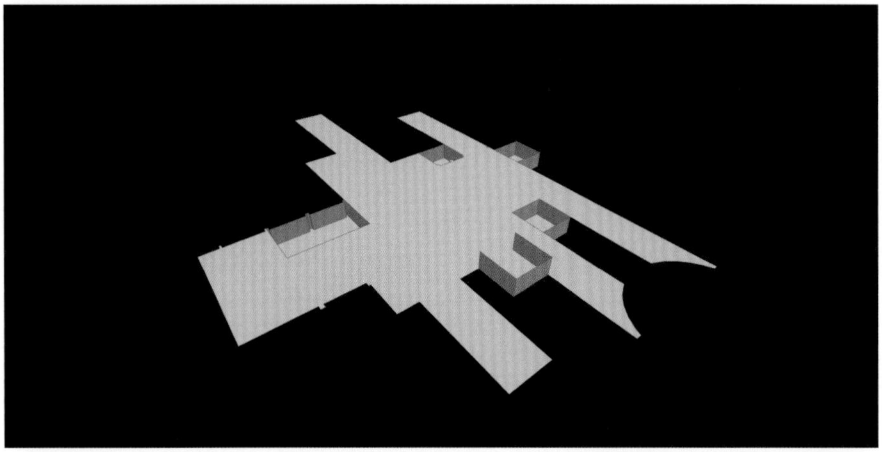
1

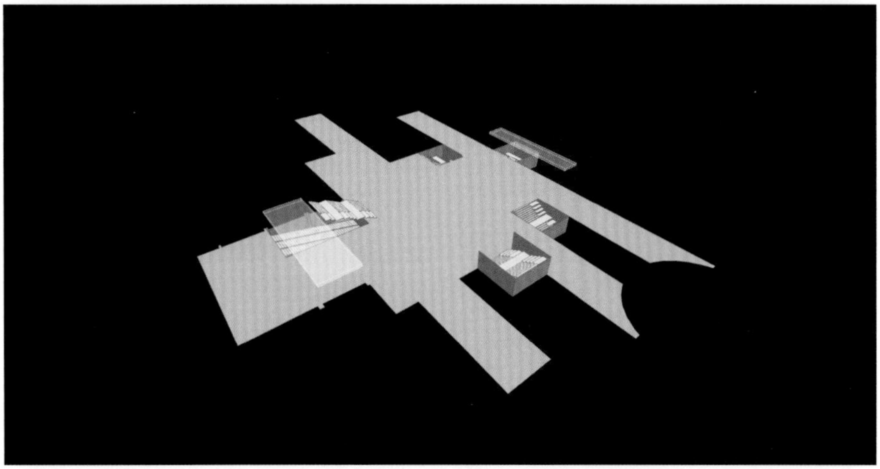
2

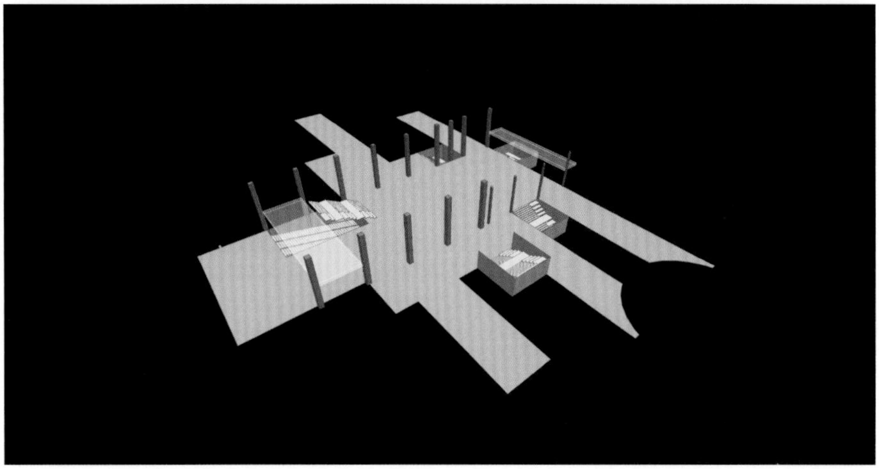
3

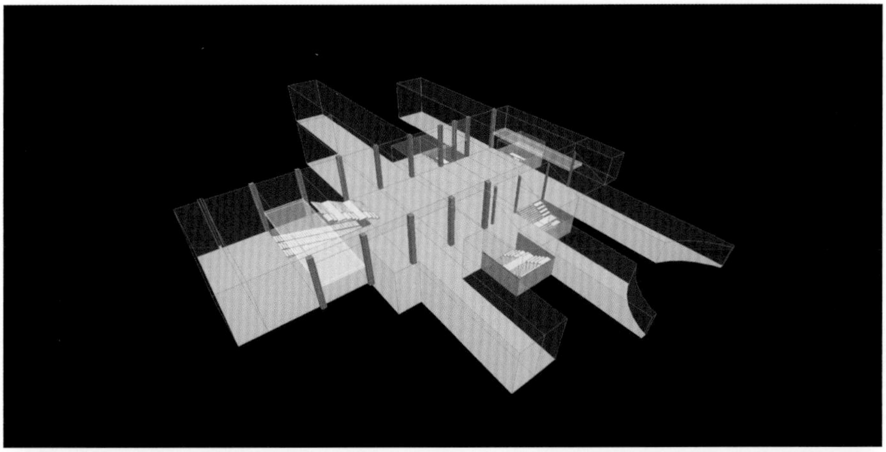

4

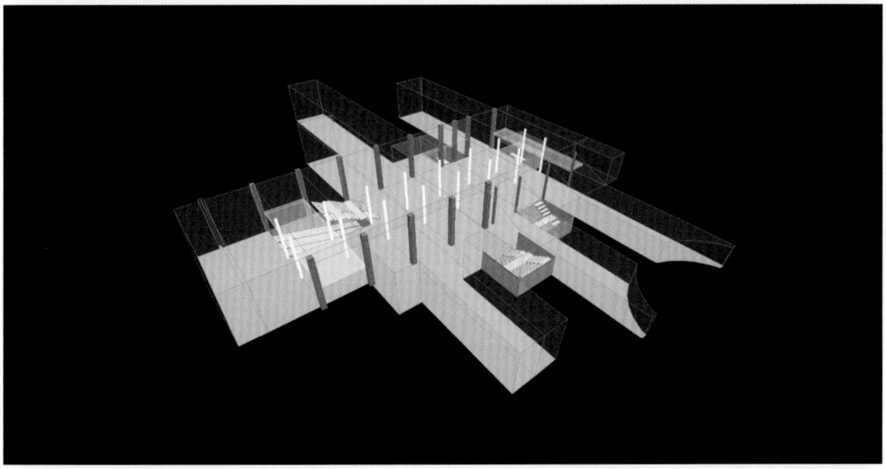

5

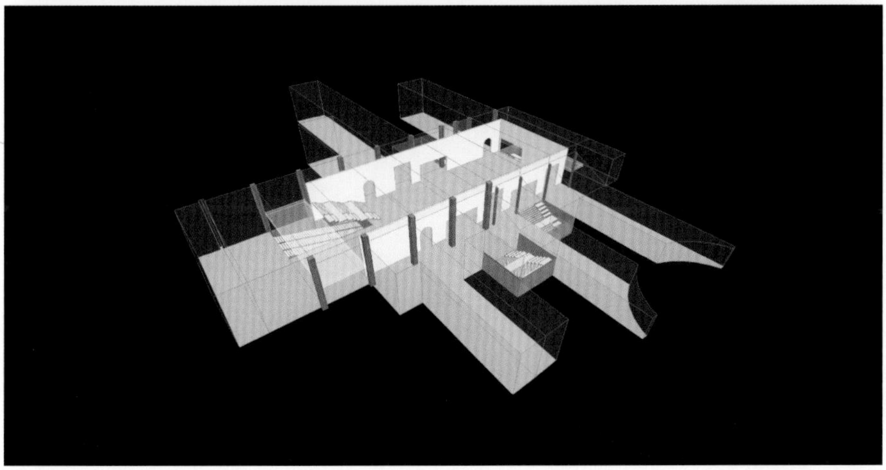

6

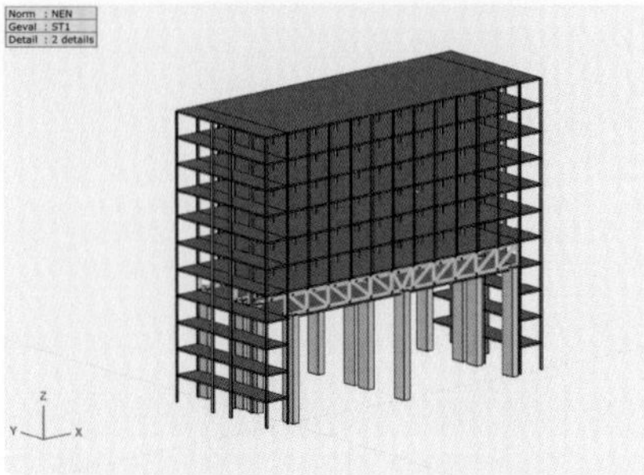

3d complete

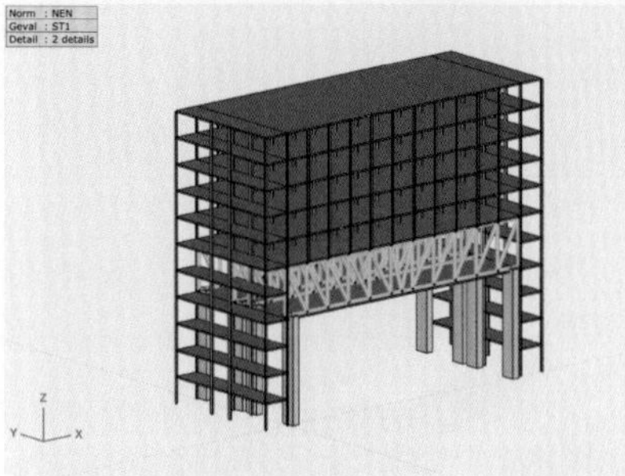

3d complete

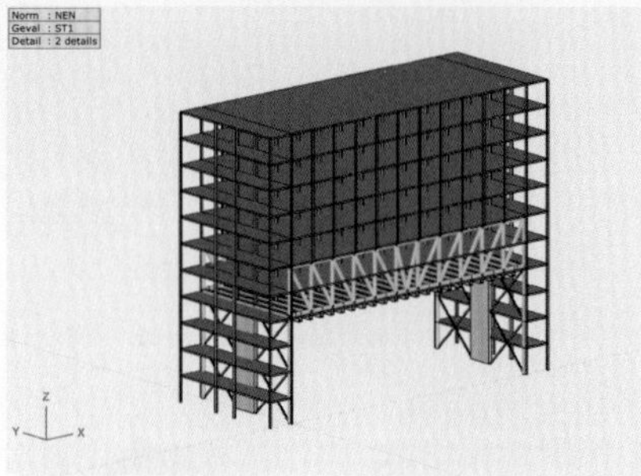

3d complete

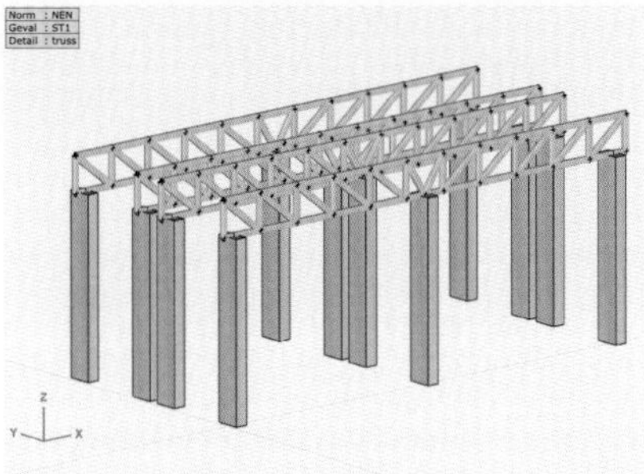

3d trusses

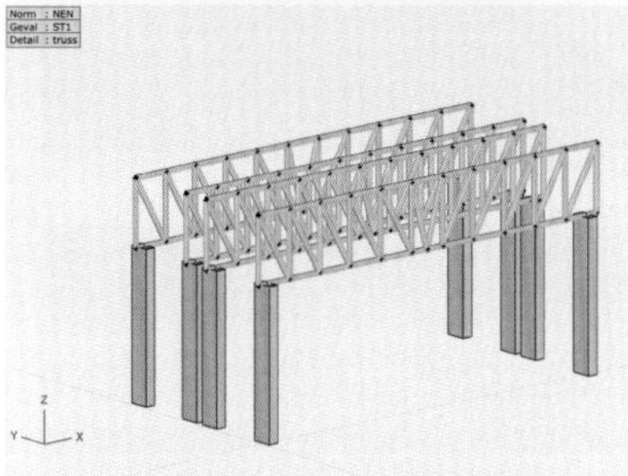

3d trusses

3d trusses

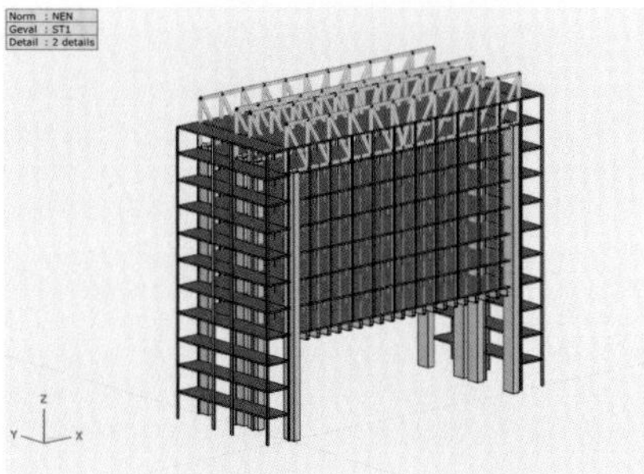

3d complete

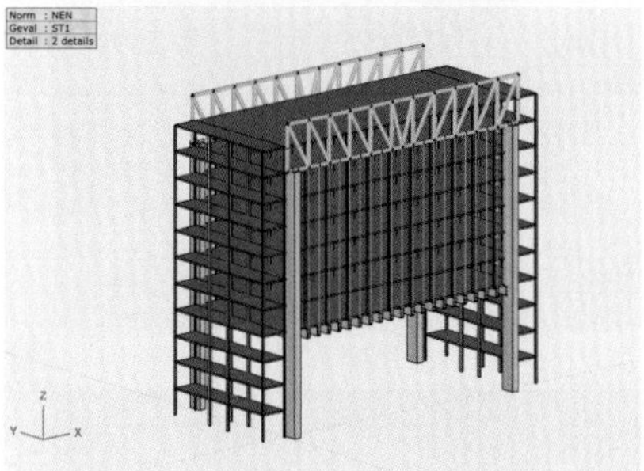

3d complete

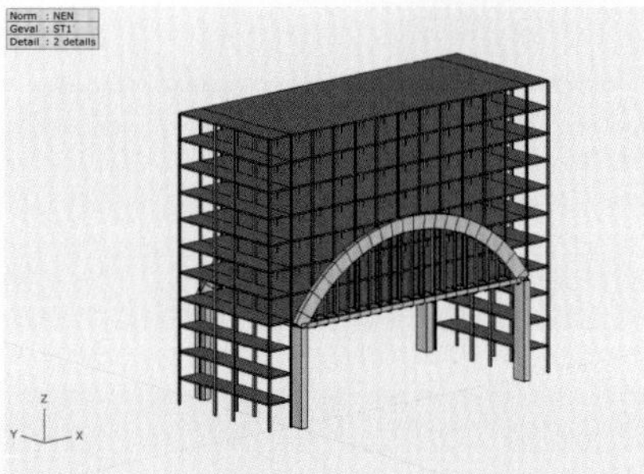

3d complete

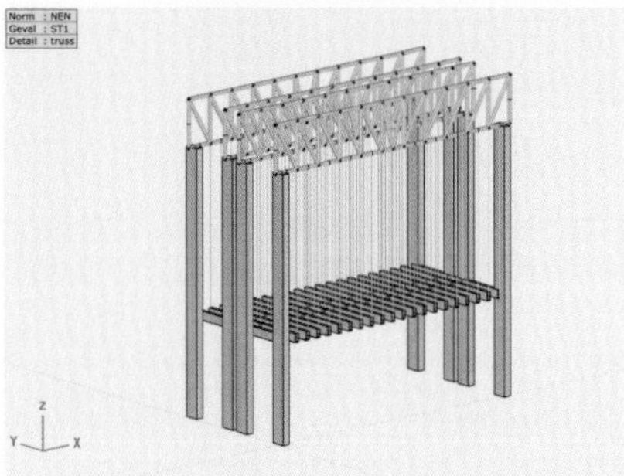

3d trusses

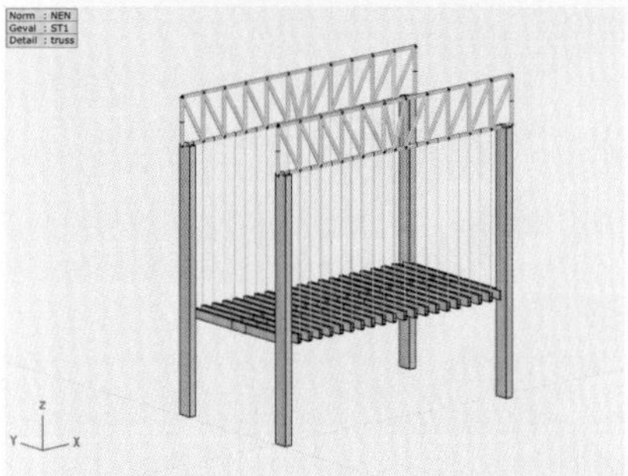

3d trusses

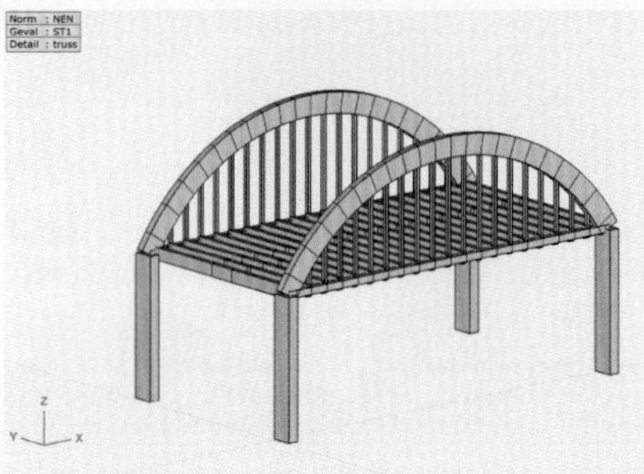

3d arch

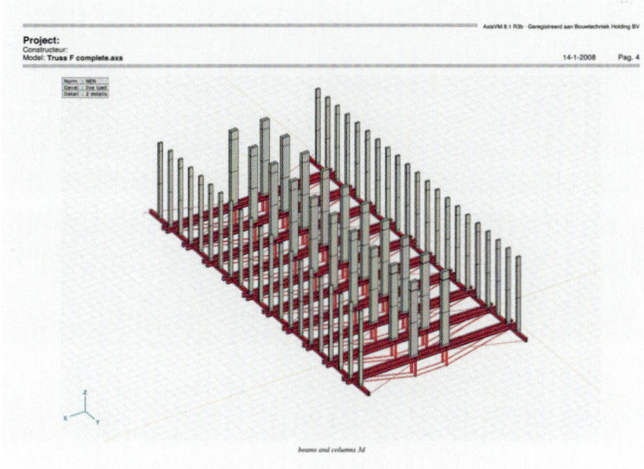

beams and columns 3d

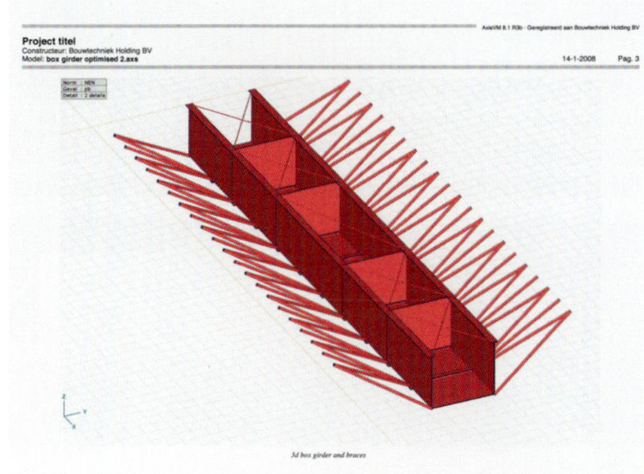

3d box girder and braces

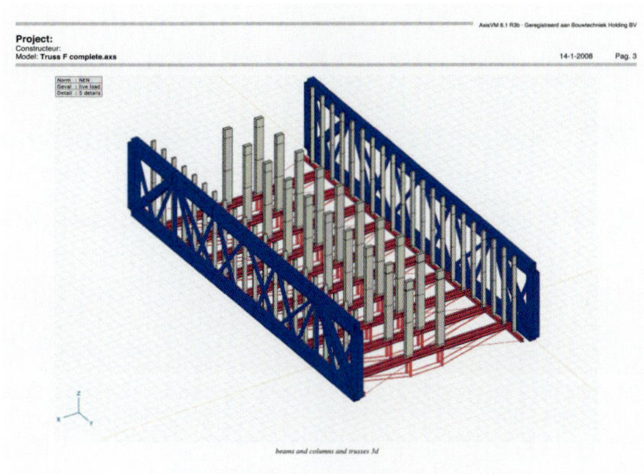

beams and columns and trusses 3d

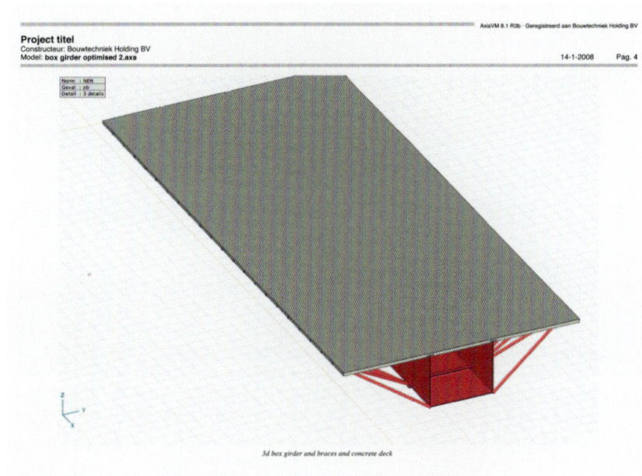

3d box girder and braces and concrete deck

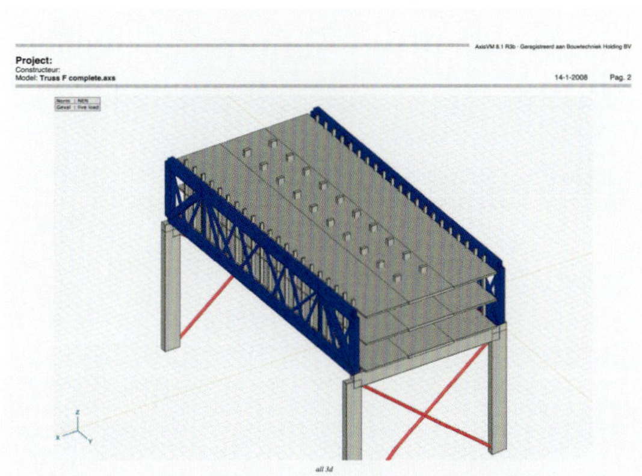

all 3d

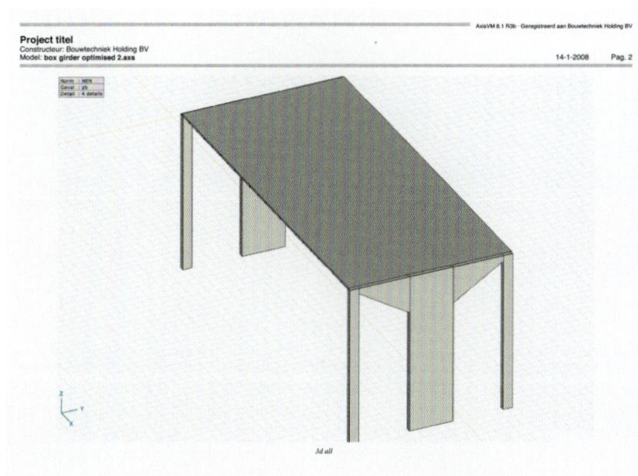

3d all

Varying structural strategies for supporting the cut through the slab block were explored. The solution eventually adopted is barely manifest from the exterior: the space is spanned by a reinforced concrete box girder with diagonal steel bracings reaching out from it to support the edges of the floor slab above. Installed 'inboard' of the structure, the block's facades remain uninterrupted.

Study models began to explore the specifics of the building in the city.

PHASE 1+

MAR–OCT 08

IN WHICH WE REFINE OUR STRATEGIC MOVES,
AND VISUALISE PASSAGE AND PUBLIC ROOMS

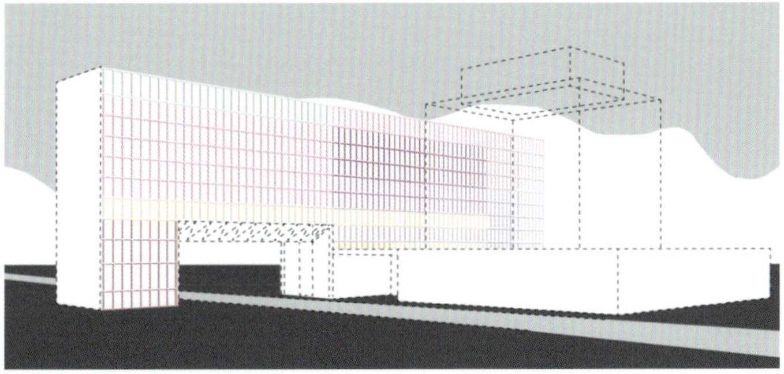

1

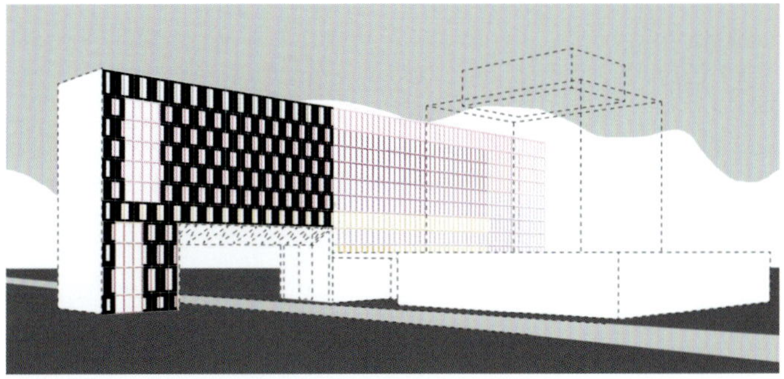

2

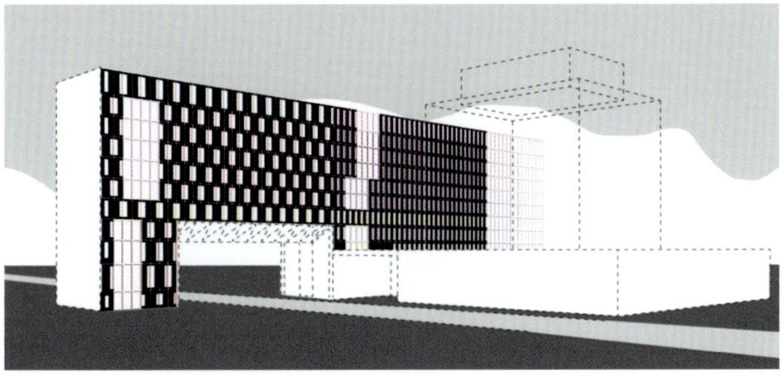

3

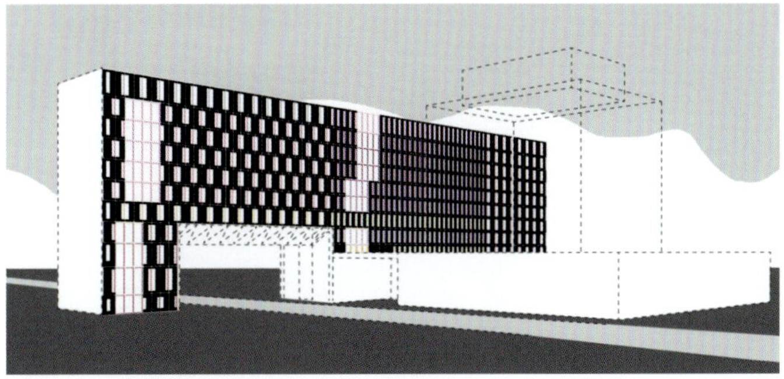

4

5

6

The main strategic moves of the project would be continually refined as the brief and project conditions evolved. At this stage they were to: identify departmental houses within the slab block with the use of internal colour (1); lay on a new facade that would allow each house to be identified on the long elevation (2-4); create public rooms and a connecting passage between the two blocks (5); and add new facades to point block A (6).

The facade design was driven by the existing frame of the building, interrogated initially by using a physical model.

Sketch studies described the impact of the block volumes on the surrounding cityscape. Other studies looked at how darker and lighter surfaces and discreetly coloured highlights could give subtle variation to the facade.

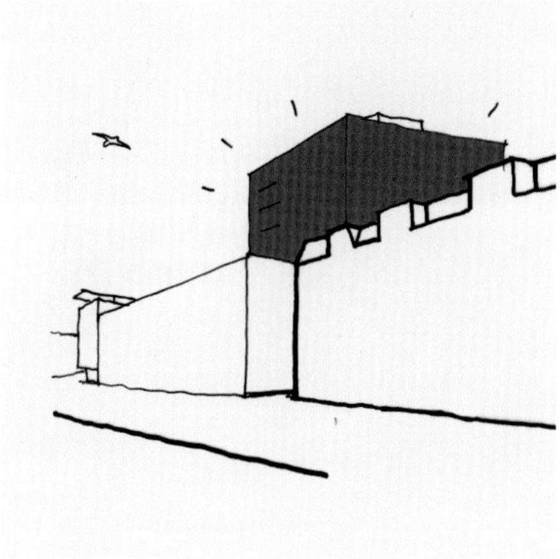
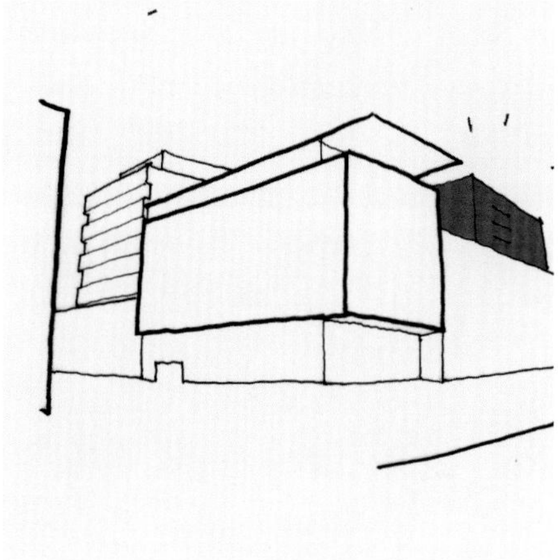
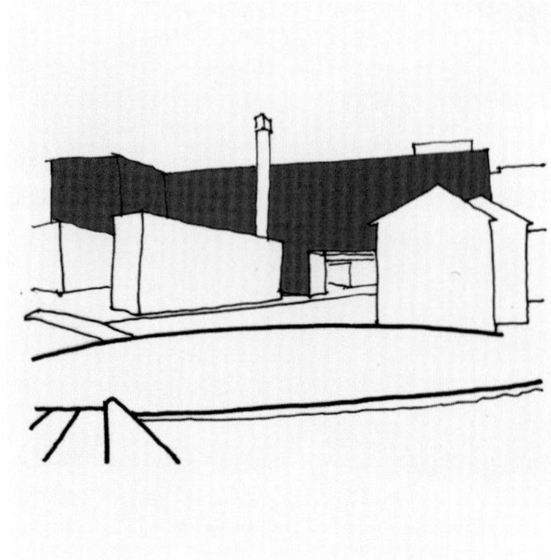

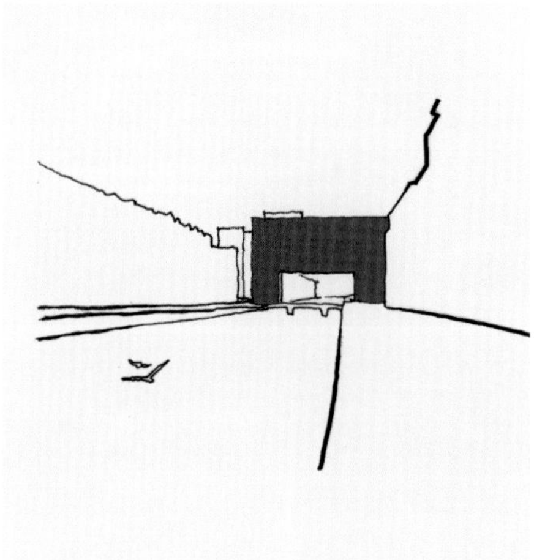
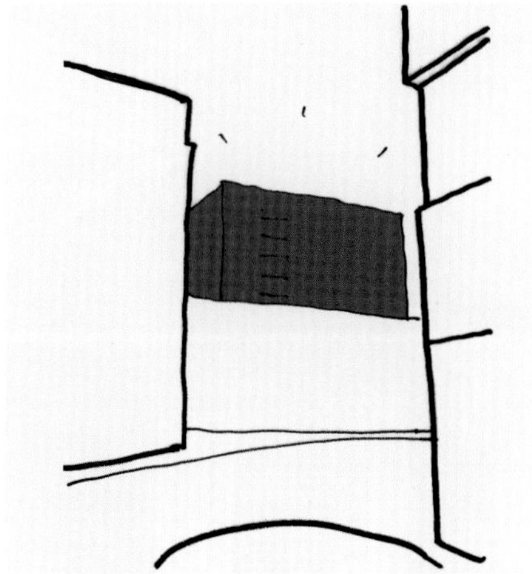

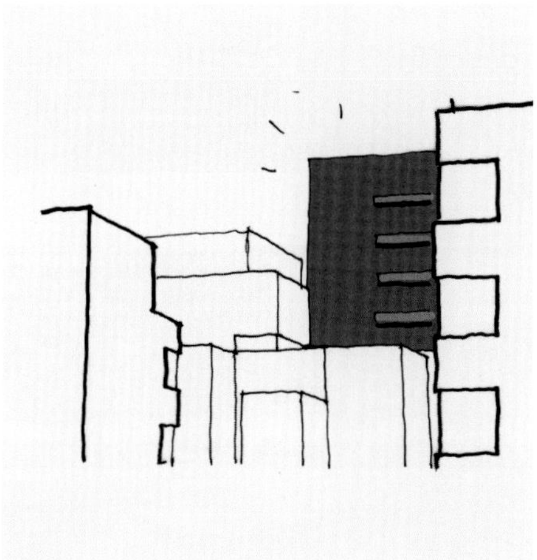
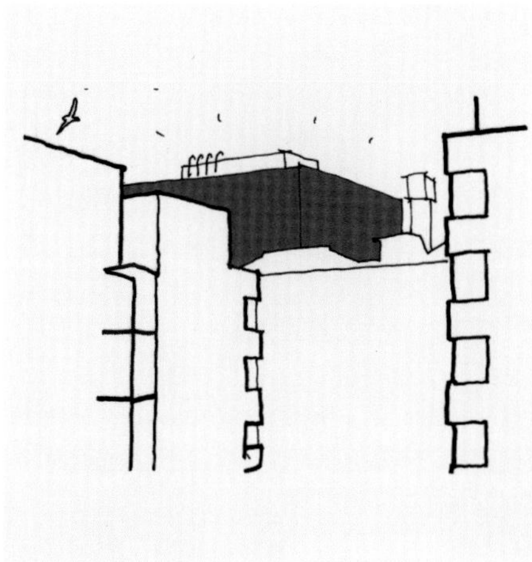

The freestanding tower became the more charismatic of the two, with the slab block a confident backdrop. Seen together, they combine the strong horizontal emphasis of much modernist architecture with the verticality of the traditional canalside buildings of Amsterdam. The podium is more transparent to give interest at street level.

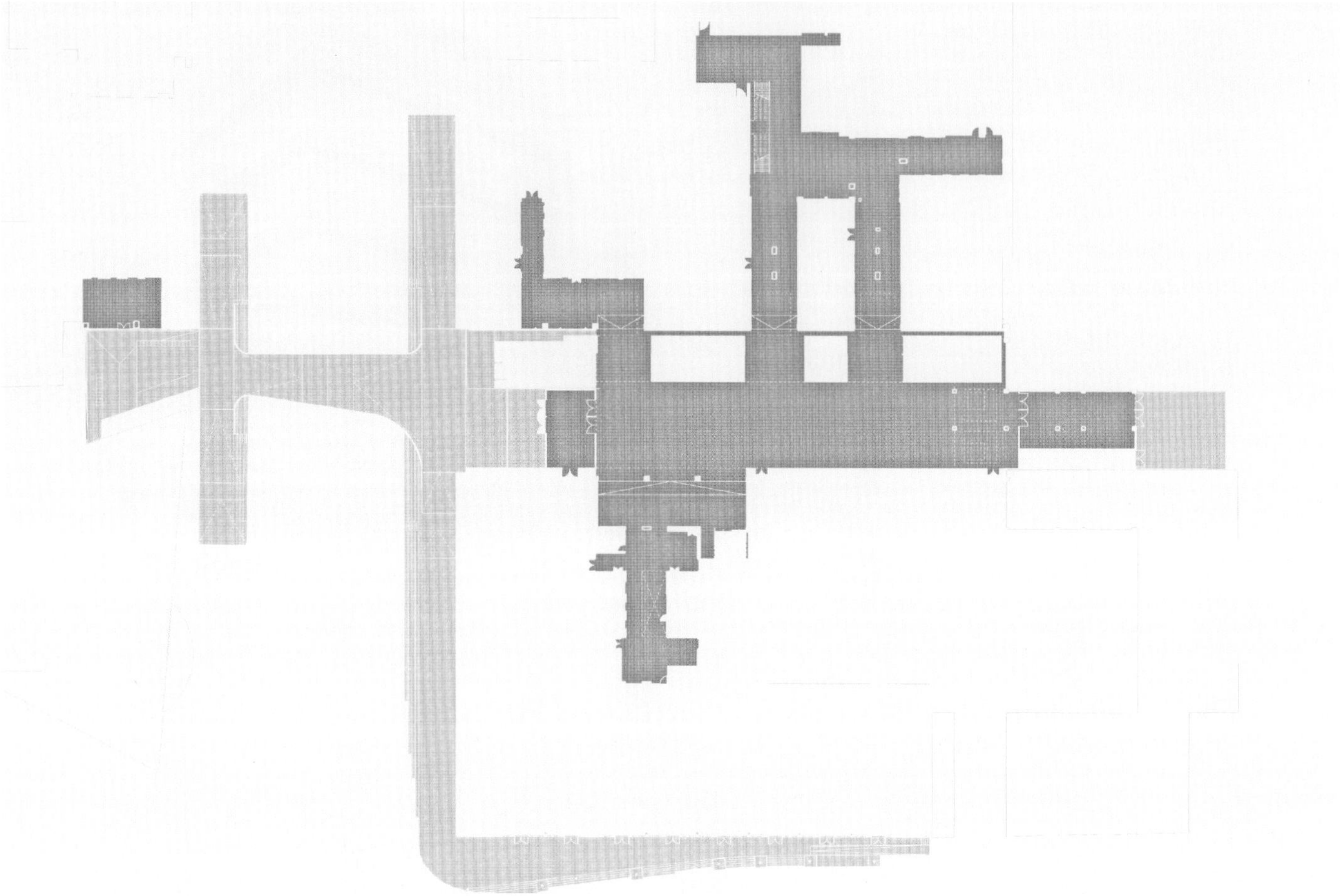

Drawn as a negative space, the significance of the passage as a place could be better seen, flowing out from the podium and onto the towpath and bridge surfaces.

Addresses within the passage and podium areas were identified as the end-points of sequential journeys from the city into the campus. These journeys begin from existing urban connections (1), and extend into the campus by way of new canalside routes and the bridge (2). They enter the building at grade via the passage (3), which is multi-layered and has further connections to the lower-ground floor concourse (4). Journeys extend over the bridge and through the passage to cores B, C and D (5), and also to the A core (6). Addresses include the ground-floor lecture halls (7), first-floor links and atria (8), and finally a first-floor 'circuit' (9) of circulation and learning landscapes.

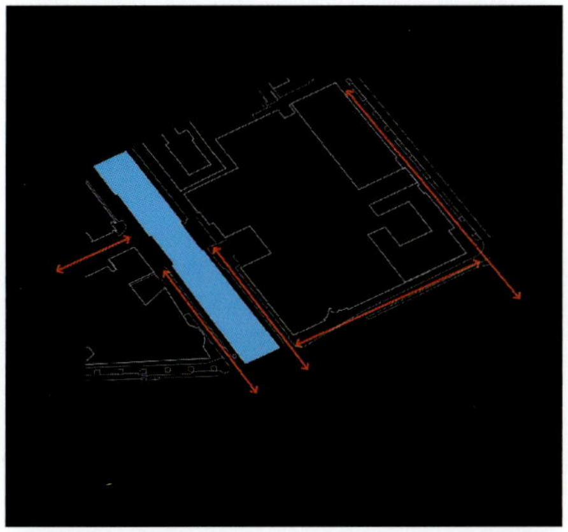
1

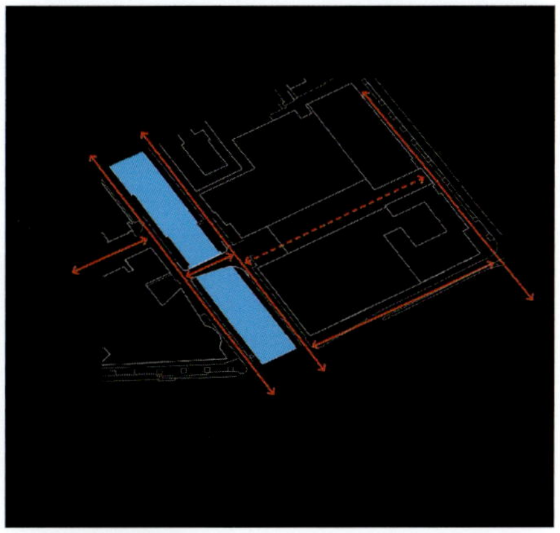
2

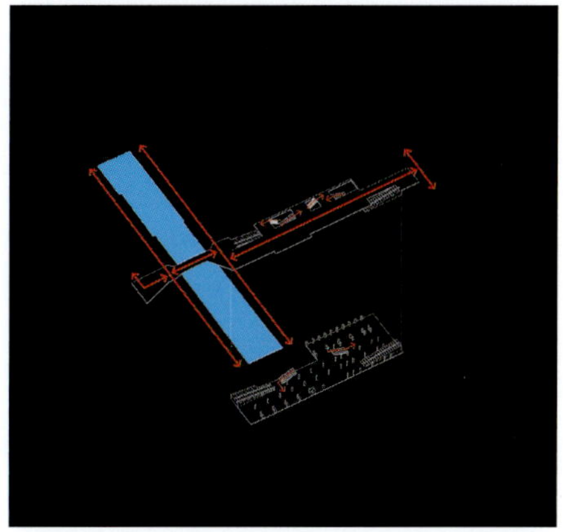
3

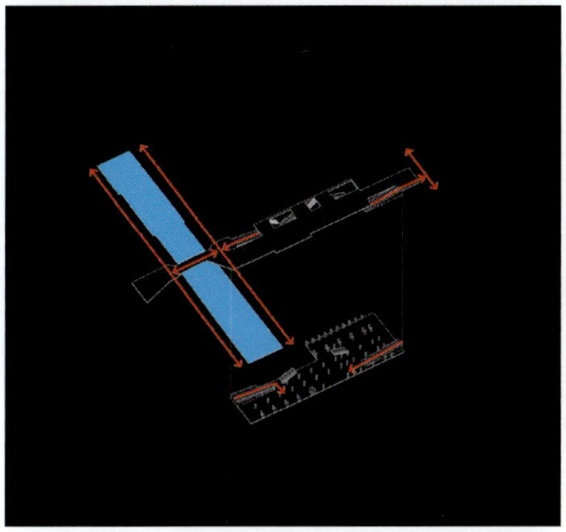
4

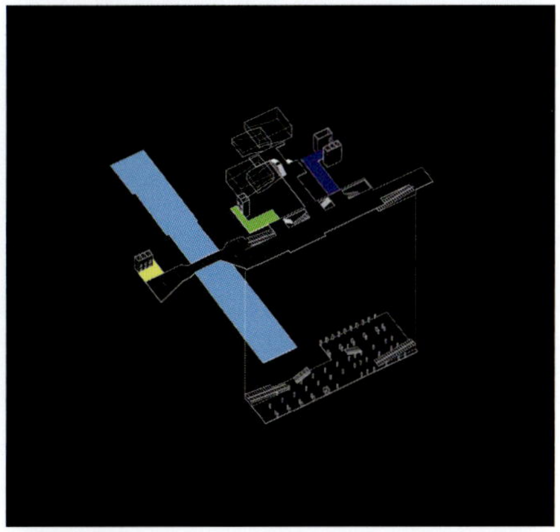
5

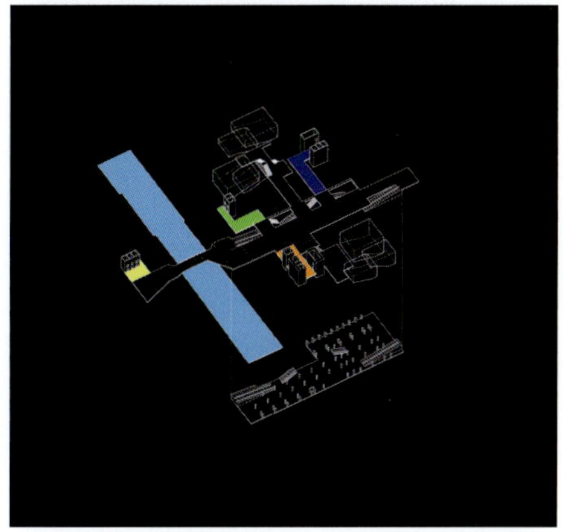
6

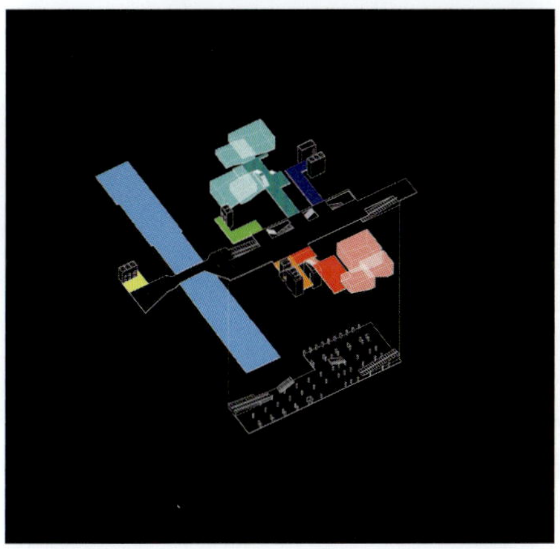
7

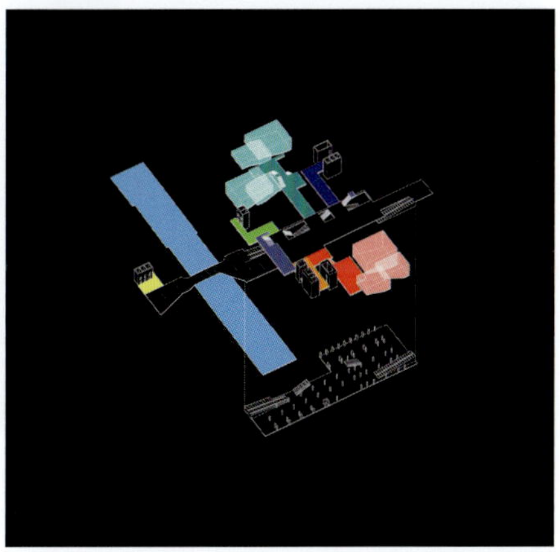
8

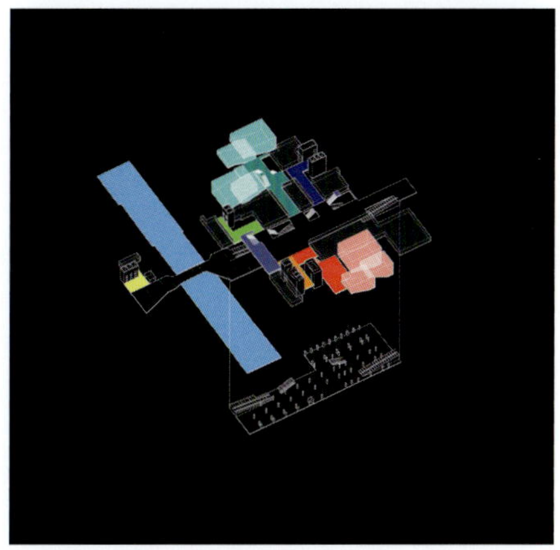
9

Oriented roughly north-south, the passage offers access to a series of addresses, arranged over multiple levels and organised into distinctive clusters.

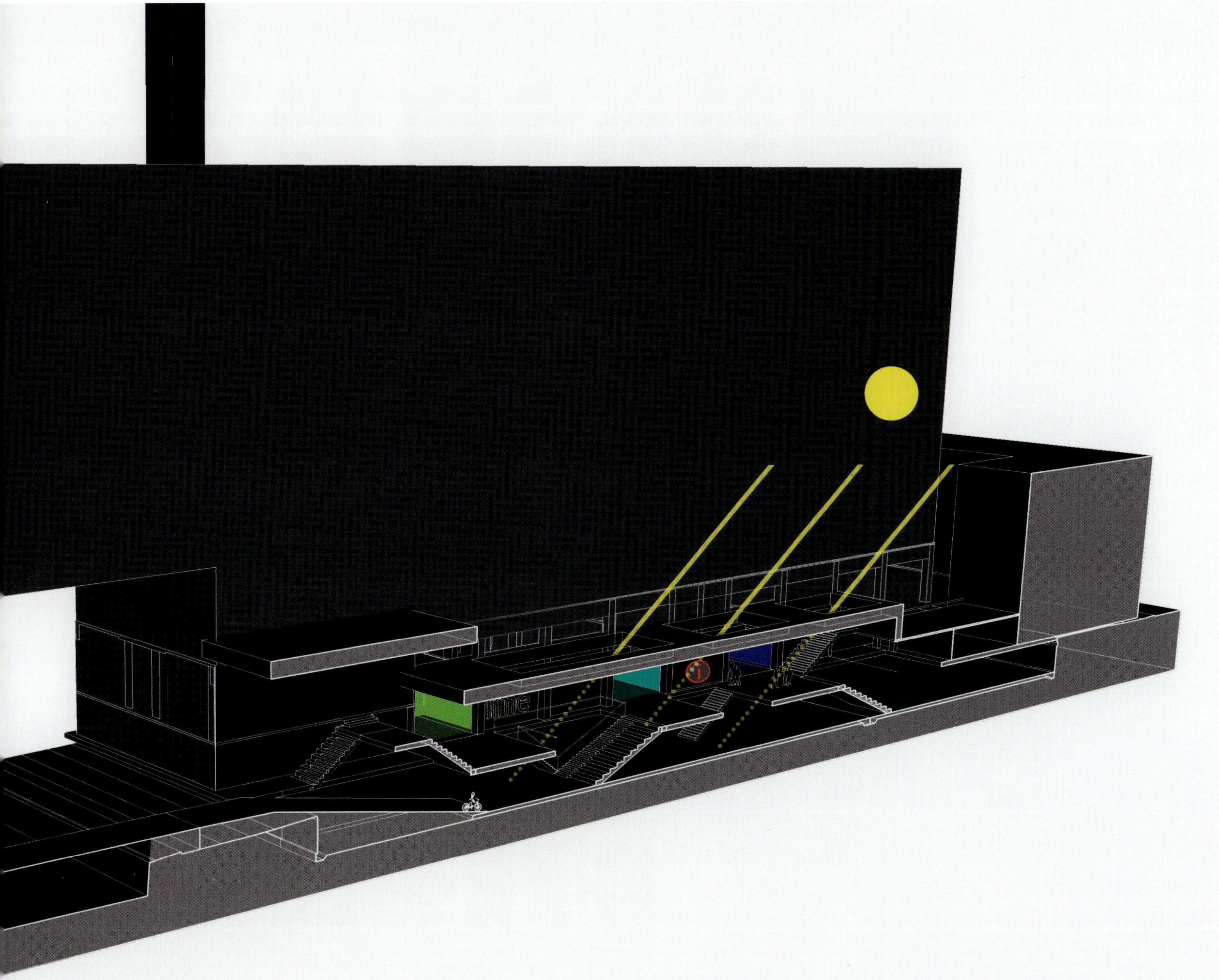

UNIVE
TEITV
MSTER

With the connectivity and purpose of the space mapped out, the look and feel of the passage was explored in more detail.

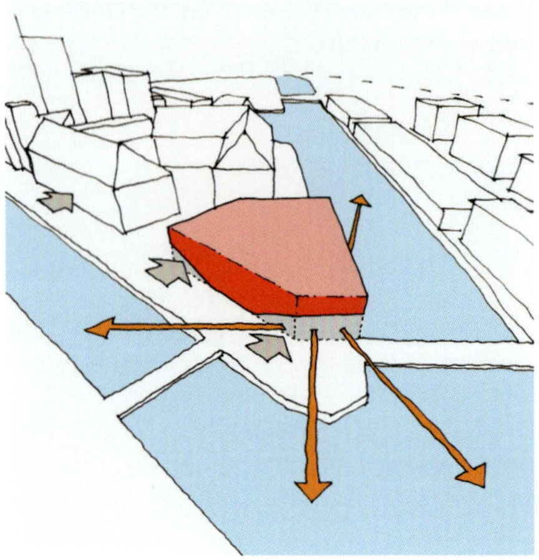
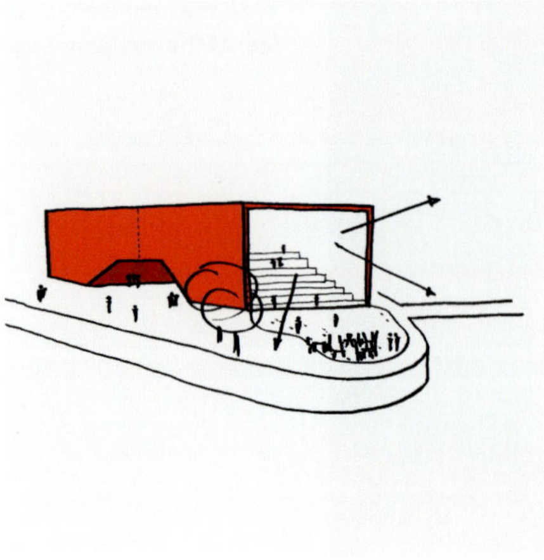
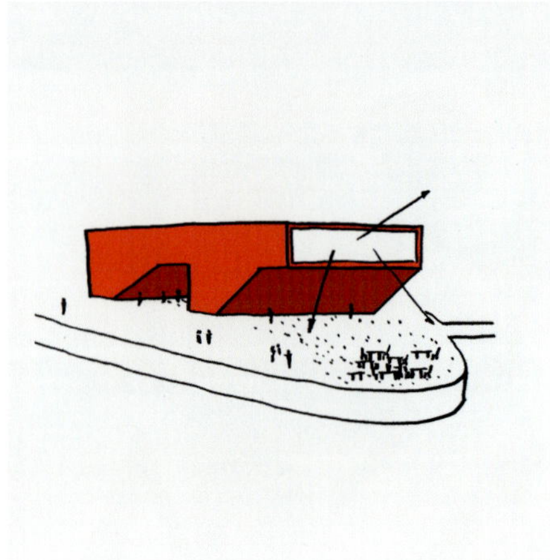
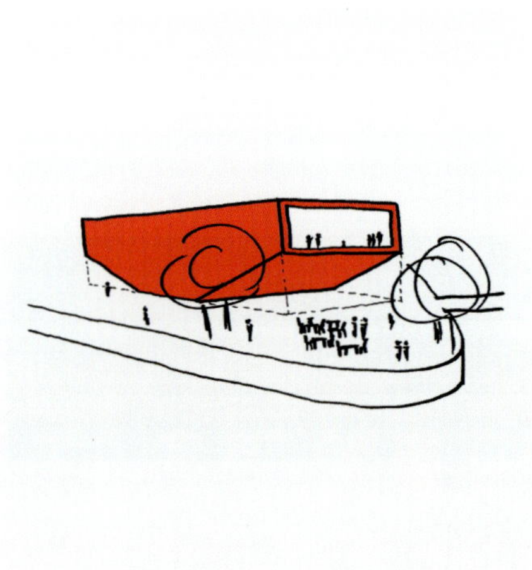
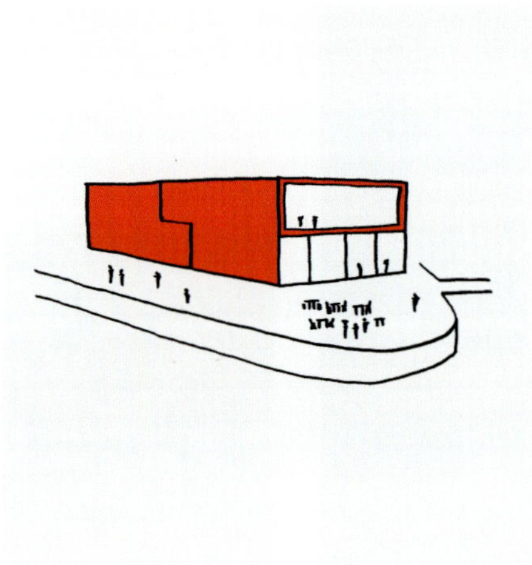
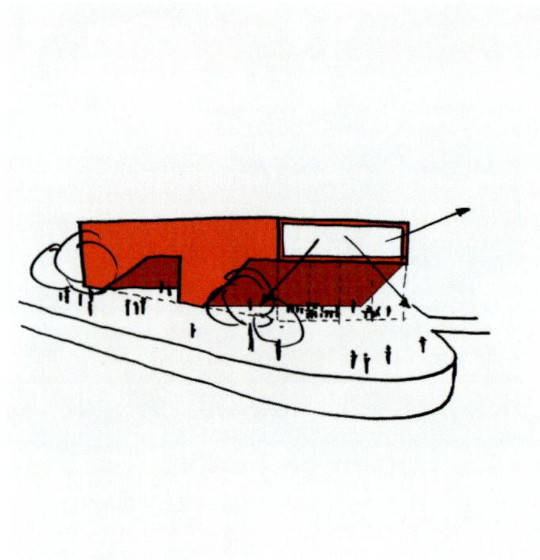
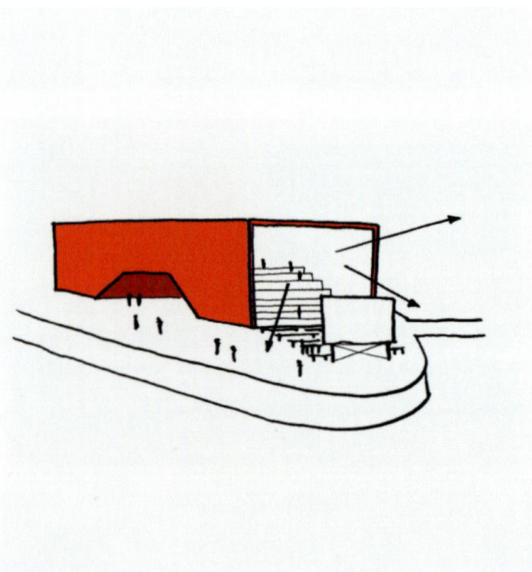
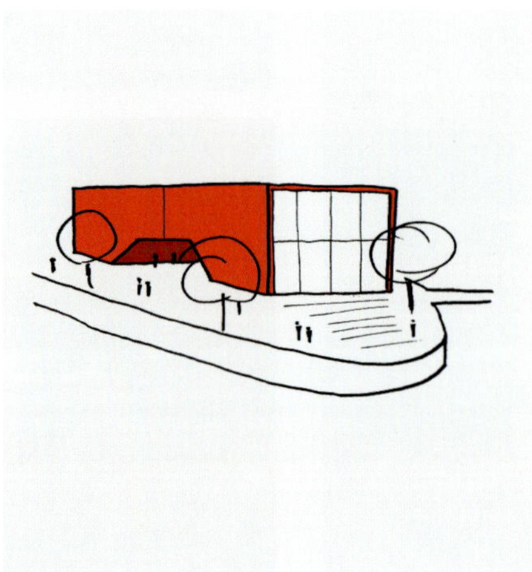

The brief for lecture rooms continued to evolve, and substantially increased as time went on. One option, later abandoned, was to build a new auditorium complex on the north-eastern tip of Roeterseiland.

With the new dedicated facility rejected on cost grounds, the brief was refined to give an intense programme of auditoria (1,650 seats across seven different venues), clustered in the podium at the foot of the tower and slab blocks.

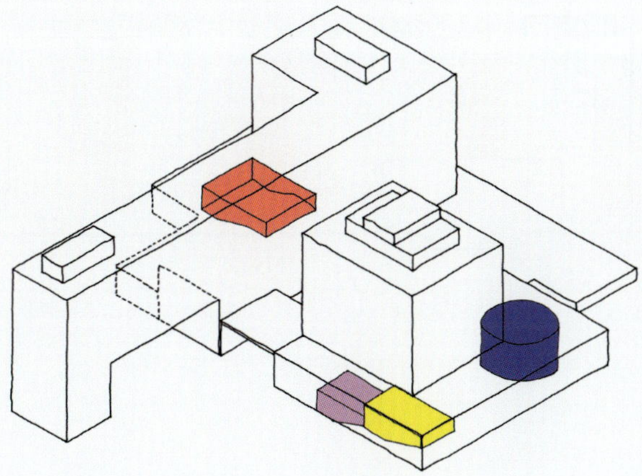

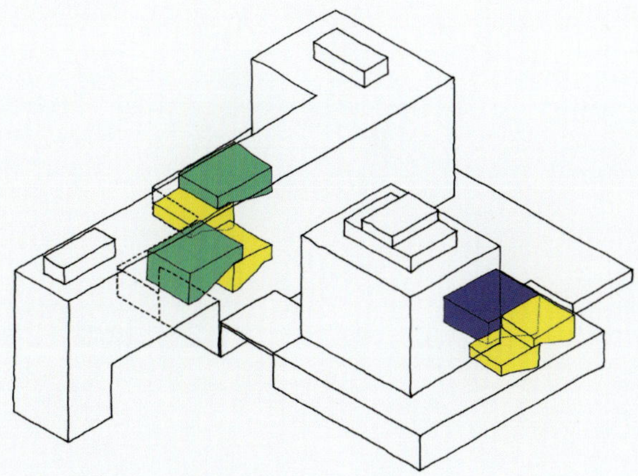

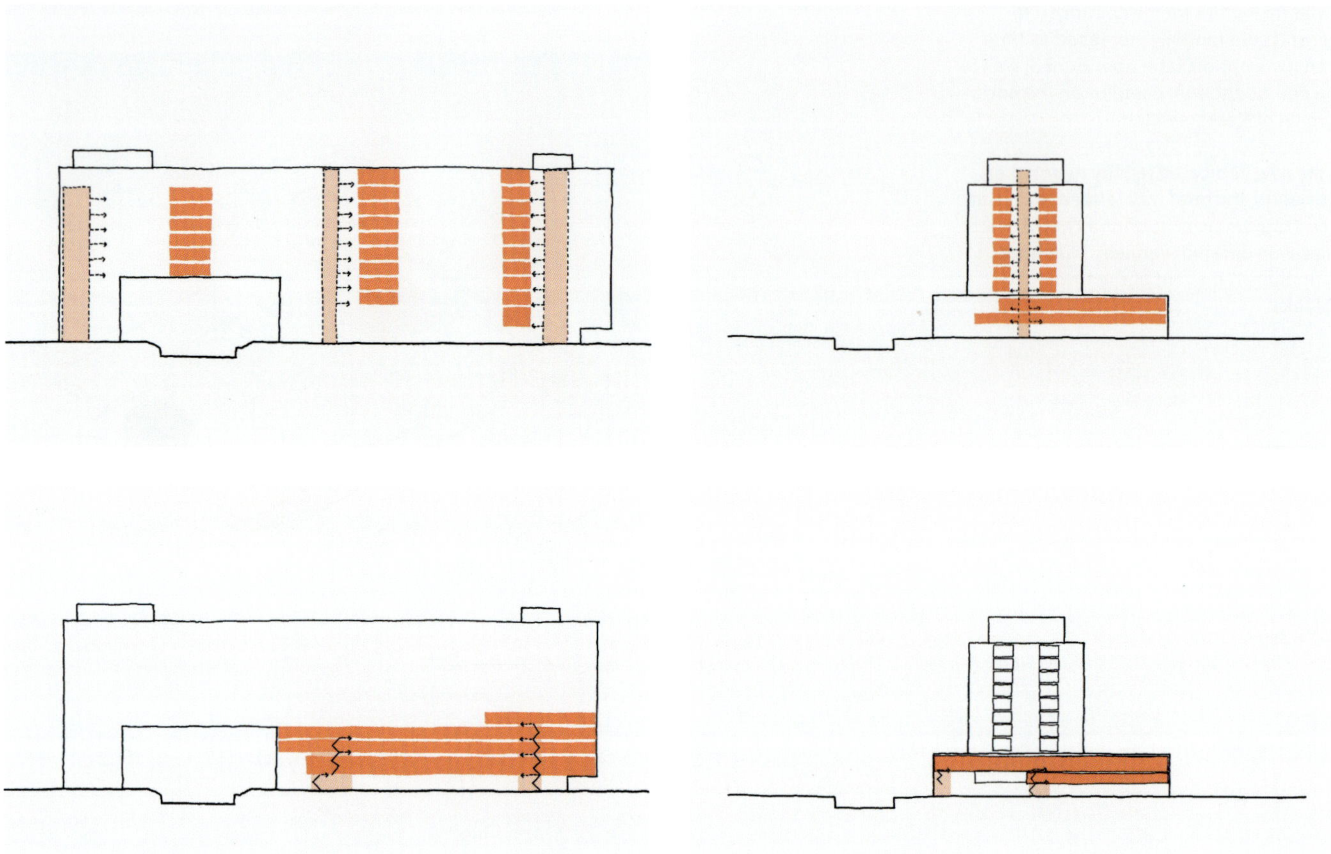

How students and staff would move through the buildings was an important issue. They could filter out across the floorplates from the cores, or along them (at the lower levels) from the passage. At this point, the team committed to putting most teaching areas on these lower floors, and staff offices in a quieter, more private zone above.

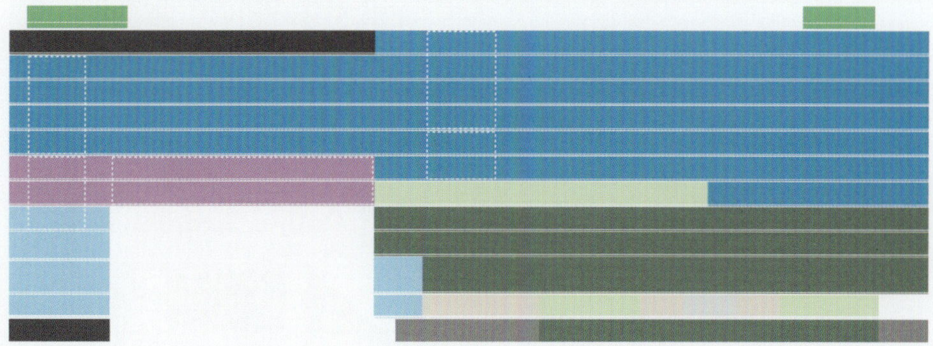

Across each floor level there would be a mix of space types: core and circulation areas, generic communal areas such as tea points and WCs, and office and/or tutorial space.

In the longer slab block, the flexible office and tutorial areas were planned as a series of modules ranked around two circulation corridors and a central service spine.

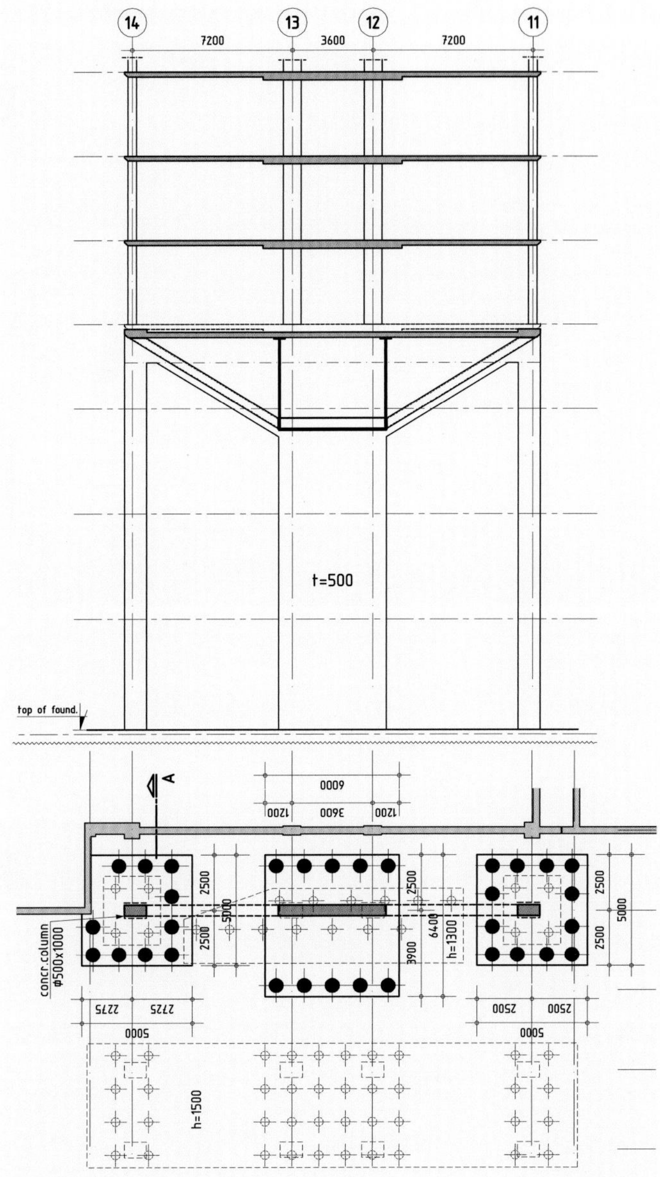

Agreement on the structure of the slab-block cut meant that the new city room above it could be visualised for the first time. The two-storey space, of more than 700 square metres, is almost magically suspended below the box girder by four rows of slender steel rods, each no thicker than a conventional 40-millimetre handrail. The struck concrete surfaces of the girder above are left untreated, and its diagonal steel bracings are clearly visible, spanning the space.

The evolving GA plans charted the increasing complexity of the brief.

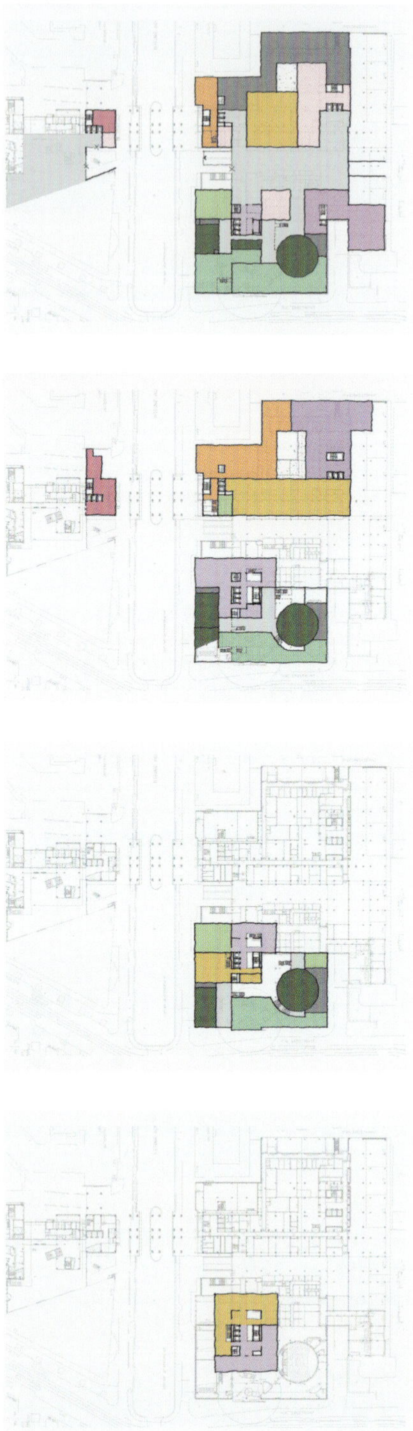

October 2007

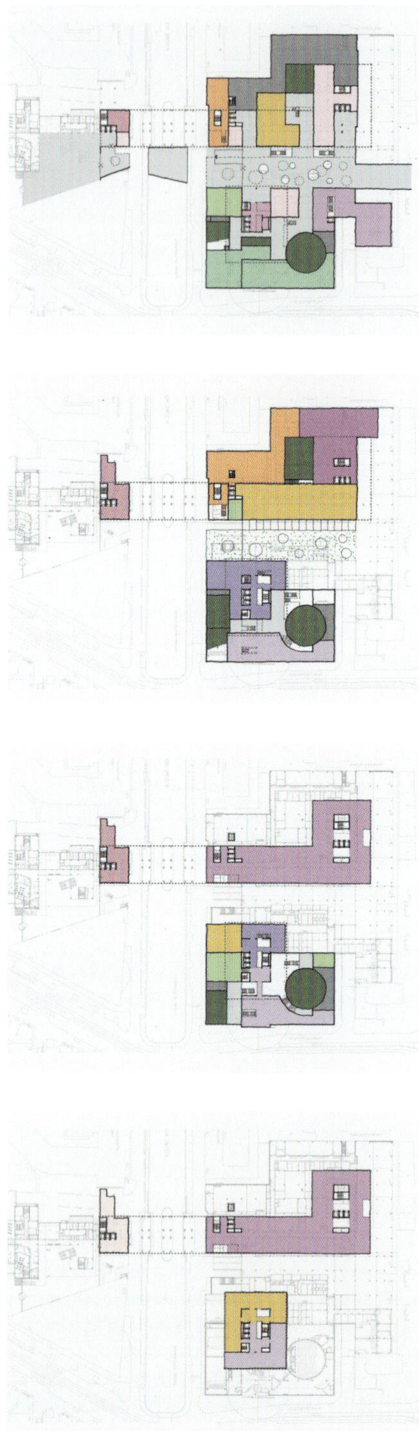

November 2007

April 2008

May 2008

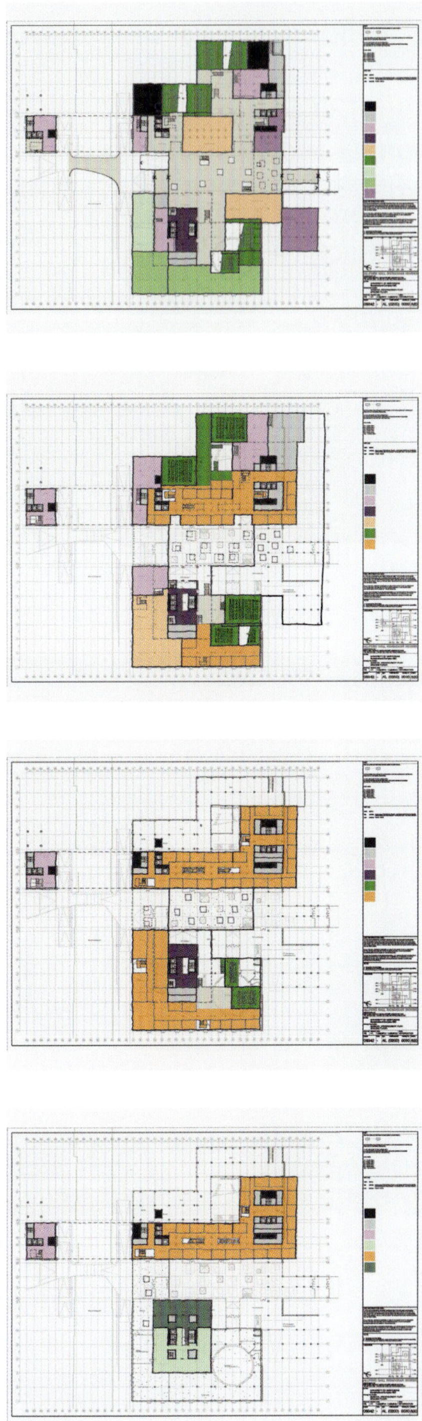

May 2008

Cut

Bridge

Passage

Facades

Houses

Atria

Lecture theatres

City room

With the city room established and the refinement of the idea of flexible departmental addresses or 'houses' throughout the building, the strategic moves now numbered eight.

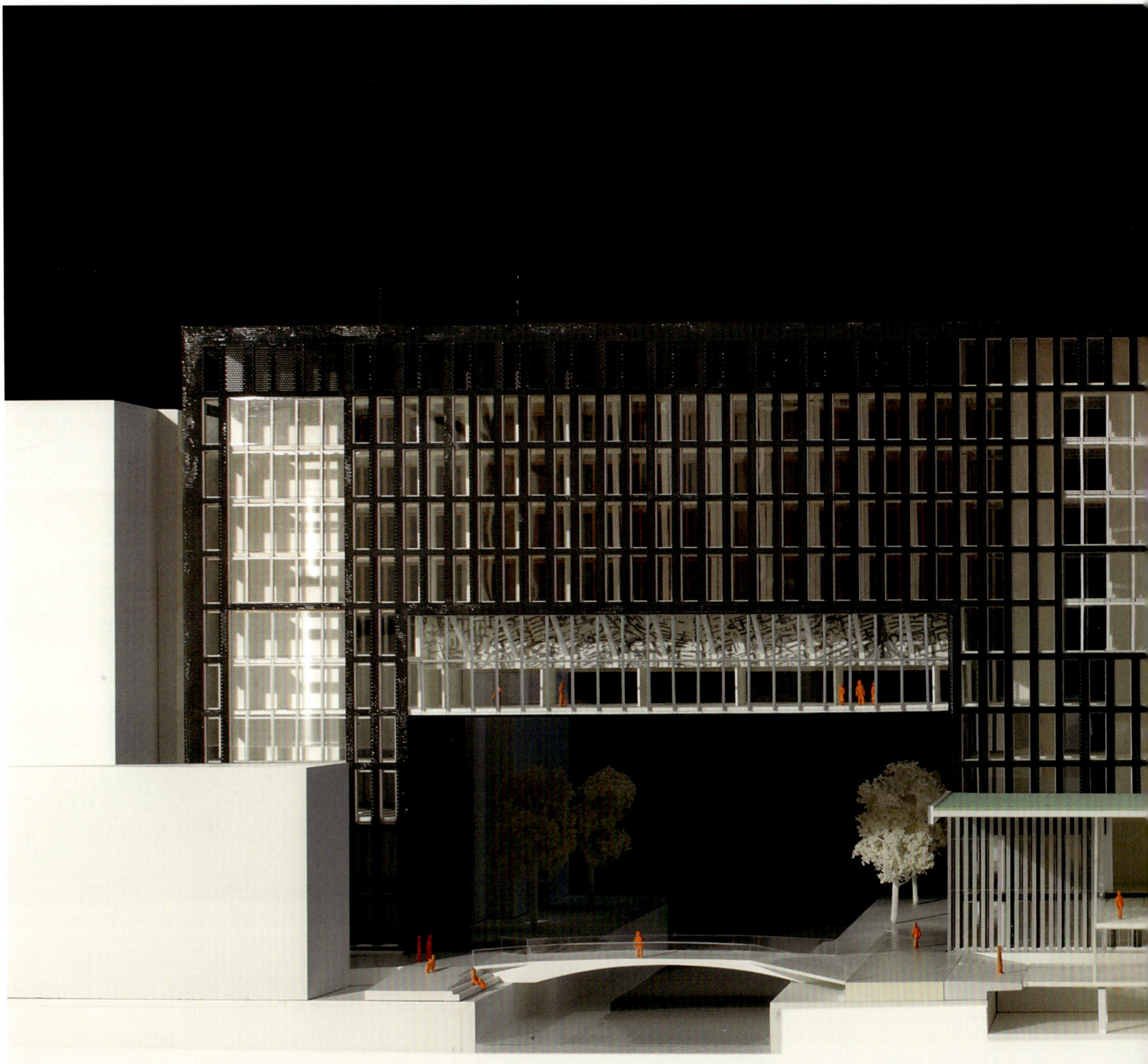

PHASE 2

NOV 08–AUG 09

IN WHICH WE WRAP AND CONDITION THE BLOCKS, AND THE BRIEF CONTINUES TO EVOLVE

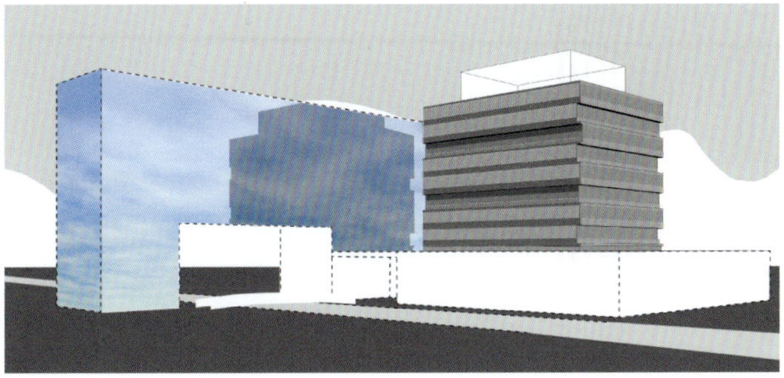

1

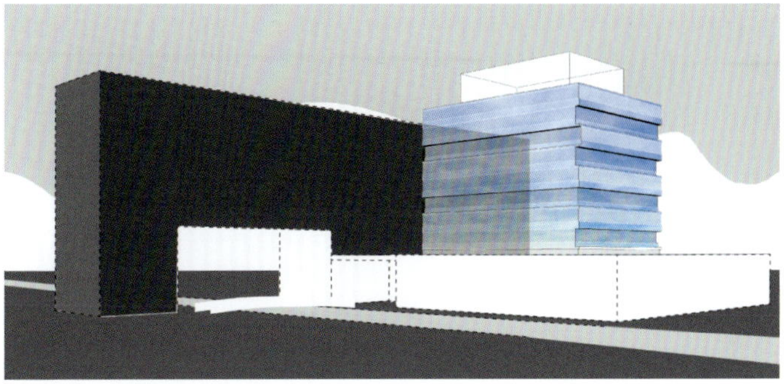

2

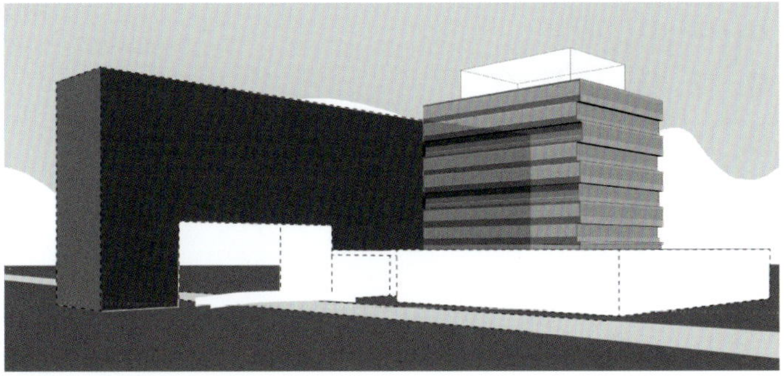

3

4

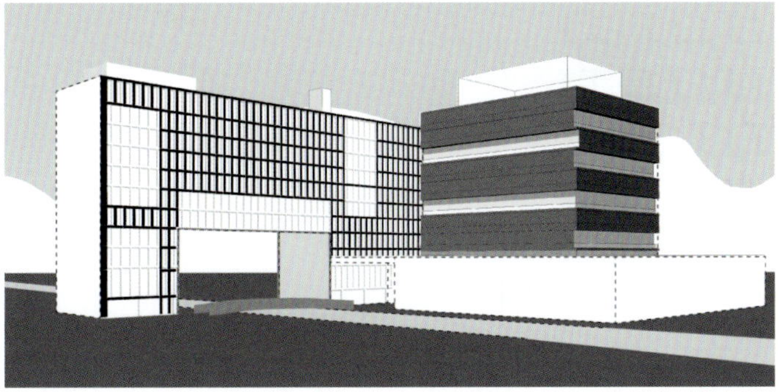

5

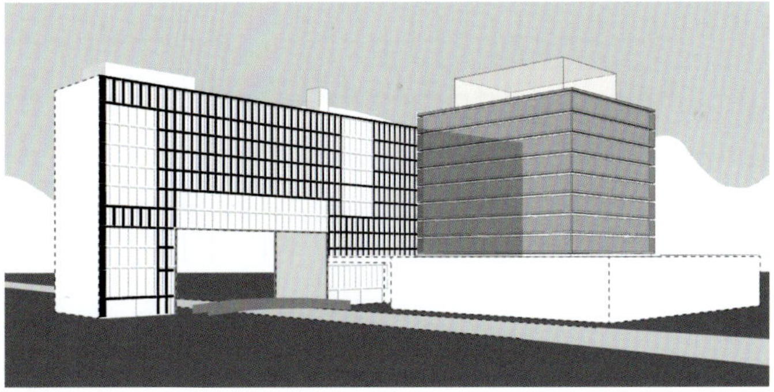

6

Work on the facades continued to treat the blocks as an ensemble of three elements: slab, tower and podium. These would be differentiated through their material, colour and articulation.

Studies looked at how matt and gloss finishes might have a shiny slab block as the reflective backdrop to the tower (1), or set a glossy tower as a jewel against a matt background (2). It was concluded that both facades should have a similar tone, with REC BC having a more matt finish than REC A (3). Pattern was also explored, as well as more sculptural treatments for each block (4-6). Finally, experiments in tonal variation (6) established that the point block would sit on a lighter podium in front of the darker slab structure.

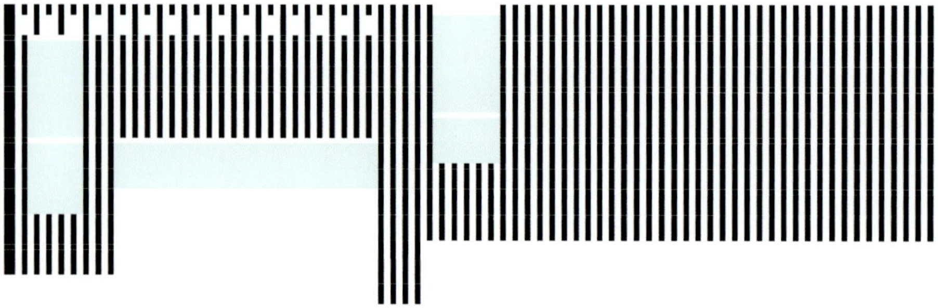
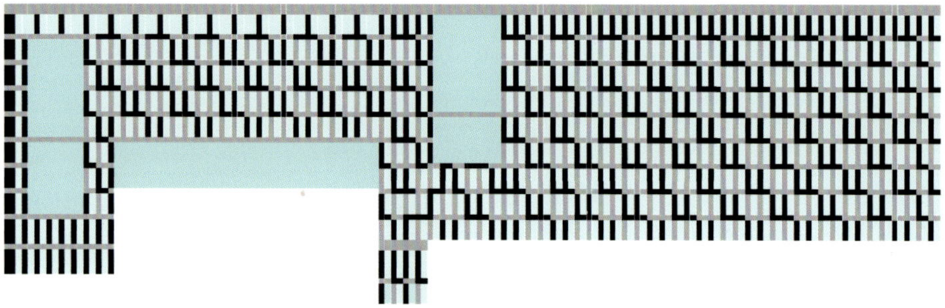
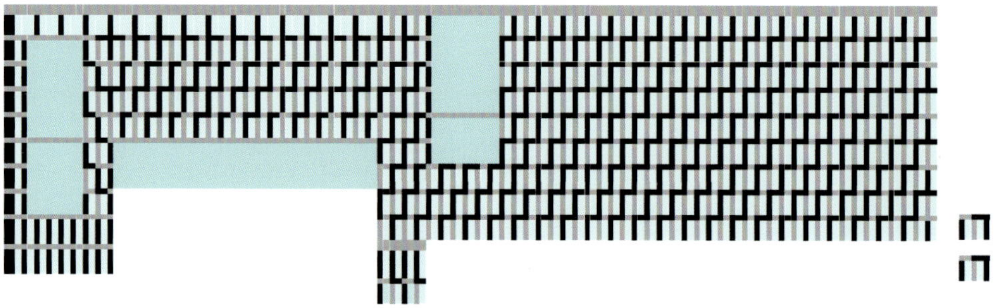
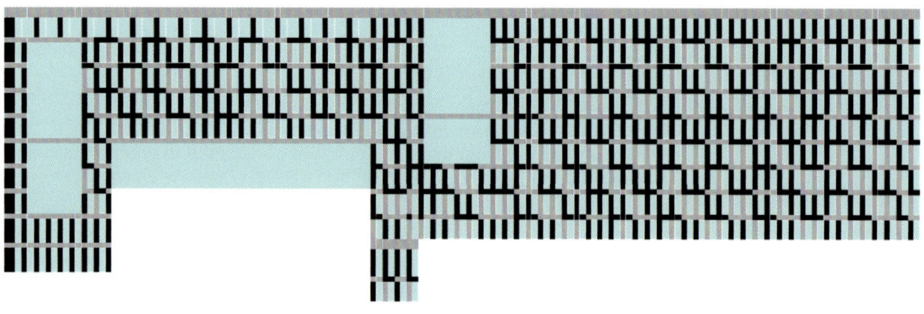

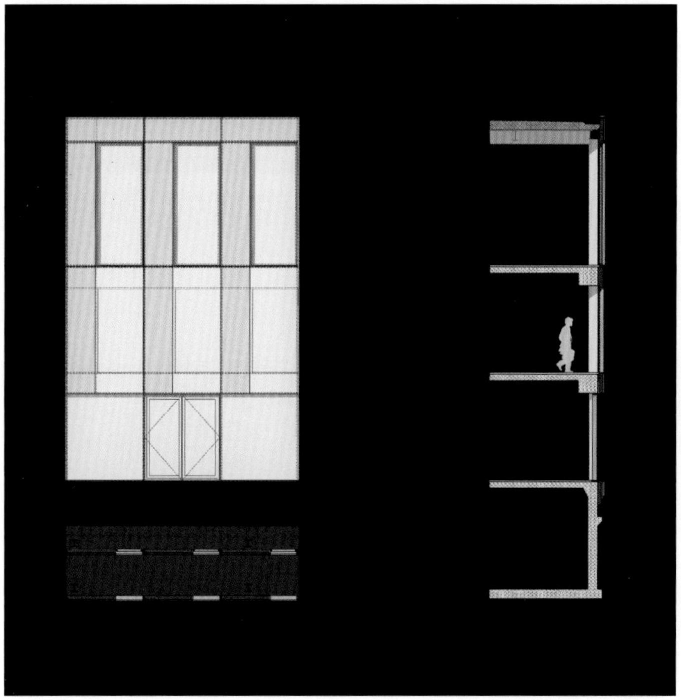

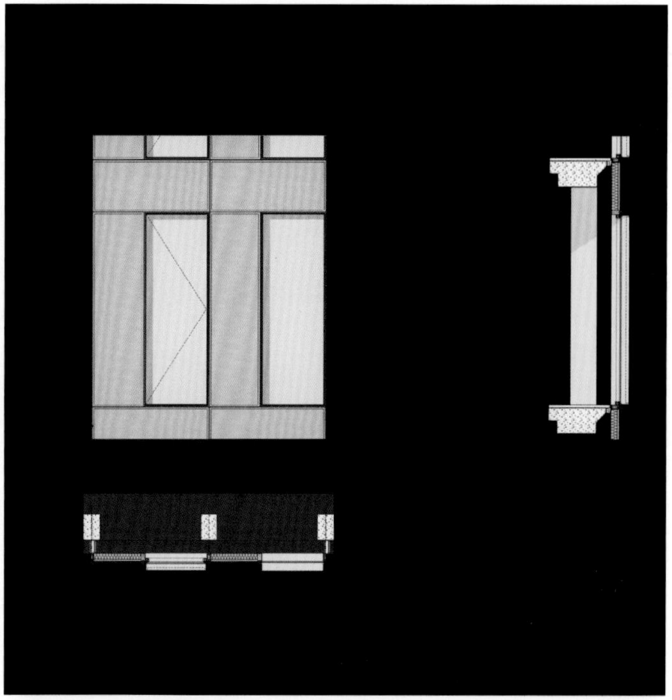

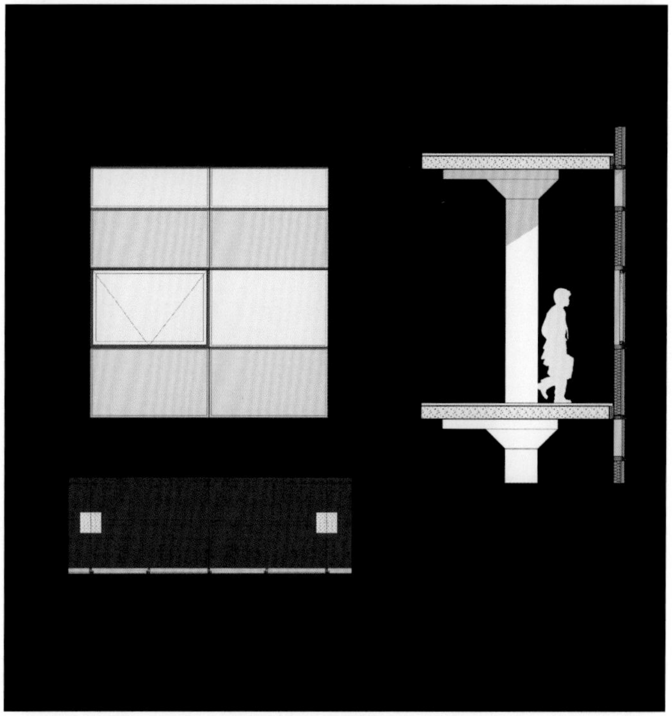

Families of related cladding components were developed for each of the three volumes, each differentiated through their construction, fenestration, environmental performance and articulation.

The superstructure of the existing buildings informed the articulation of their new facades.

The tower block had layers of projecting concrete floorplates, supported by recessed concrete columns with a much wider 7.2-metre module. This horizontality was maintained in the new facade and emphasised with a double strip of windows to each floor at high and low level. The layers of windows are stretched across a taut, black reflective surface with projecting bronze profiles.

The concrete frame of the slab block has a perimeter column grid that established the array of 1.8-metre modules across the facade. Each module has a subtly different treatment depending on the accommodation behind. This differentiation is achieved by alternating opaque- and matt-finished aluminium panels, introducing differing degrees of reflectivity, and giving certain windows slender projecting surrounds.

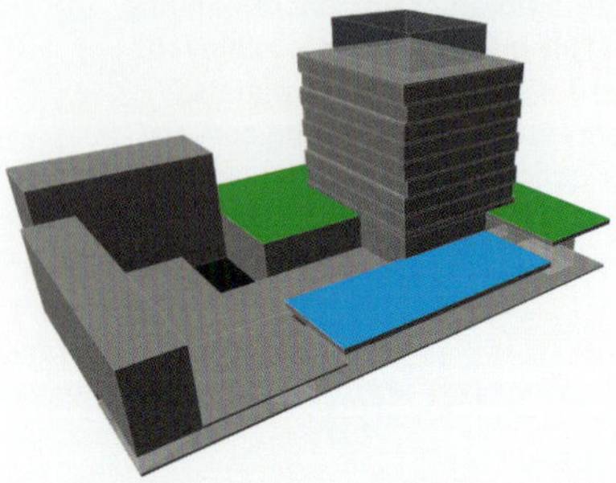

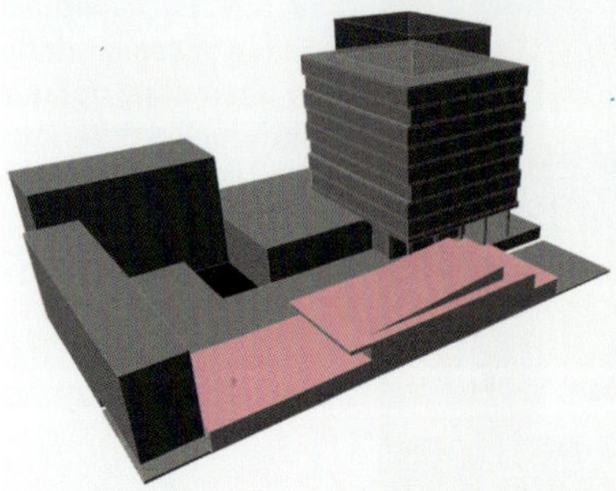

The mass of the original structure (shown in pink to the left) was a single storey, stepping back with very little presence on the canal. The city zoning plan, adopted following the masterplan revisions, suggested a much larger, three-storey structure onto the canal, but very much shallower at the back (green). Further iterations (orange and blue) challenged the zoning plan, negotiating for a two-storey passage to link the existing blocks.

Graphic studies of the passage explored its massing, volume and entrance, its comparative scale and sense of arrival.

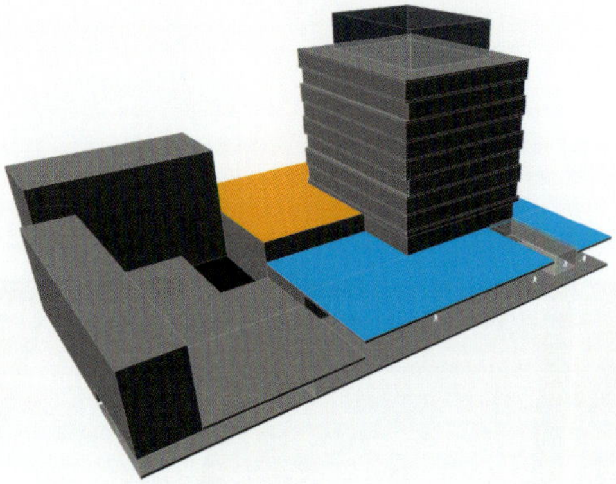

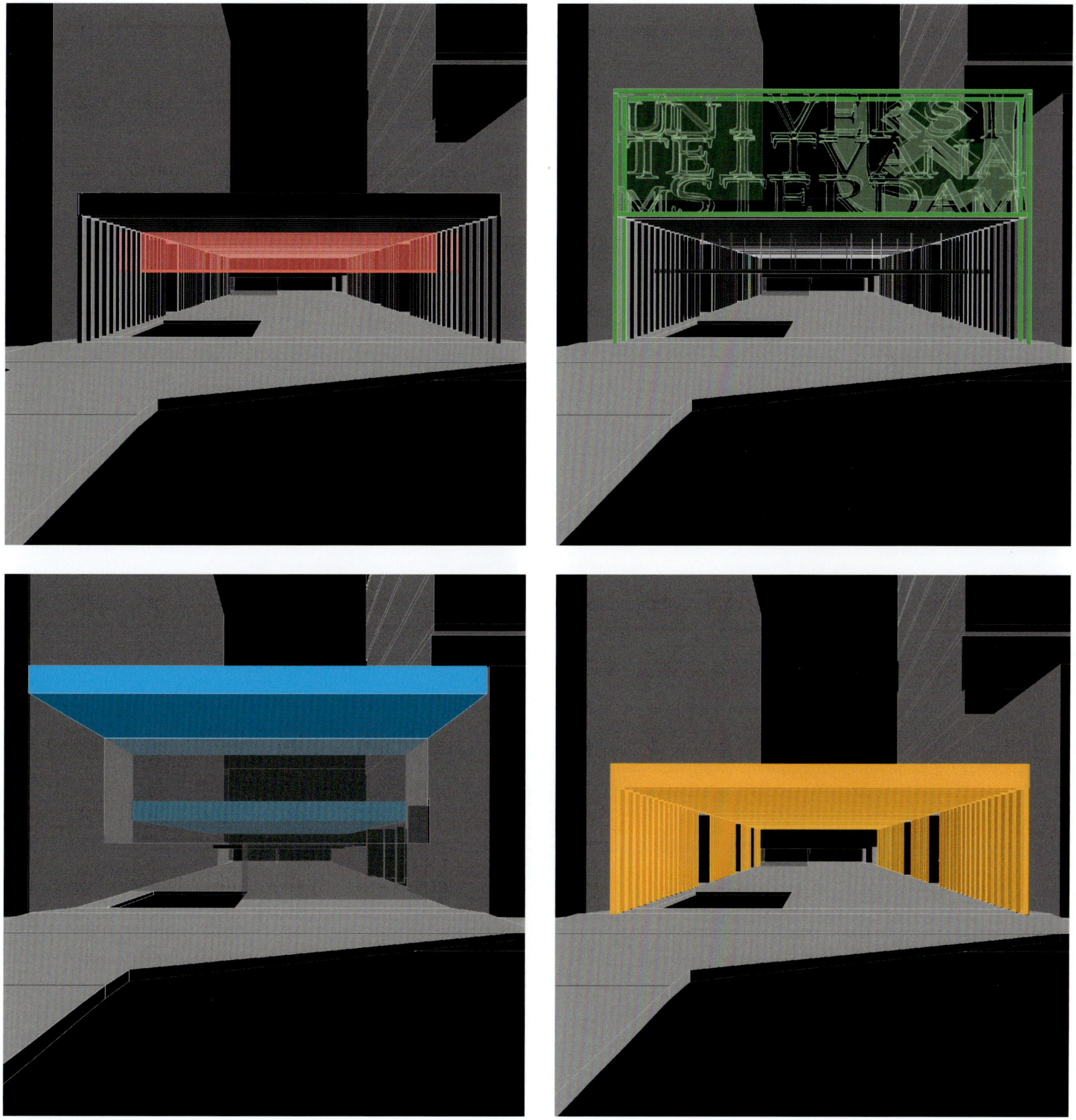
UNIVERSI
TEITVANA
MSTERDAM

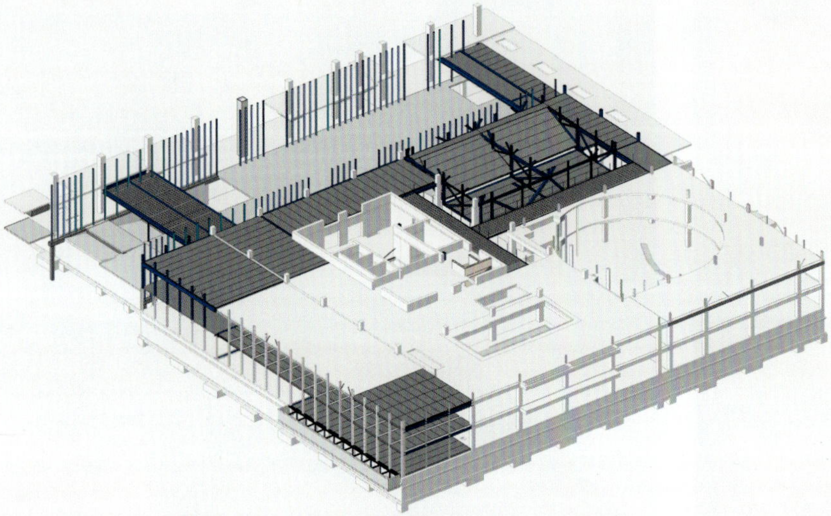

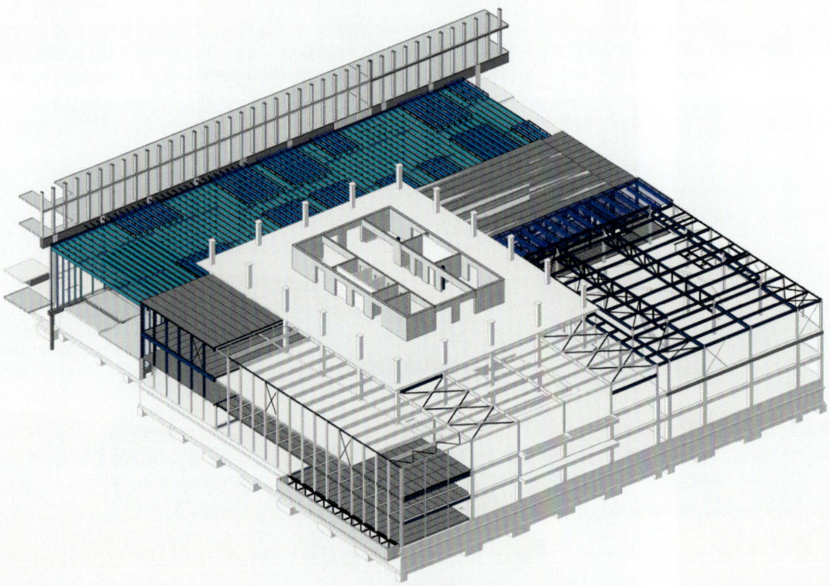

With the massing of the passage developed, detailed studies looked at how the new interventions into the podium could be engineered. Careful surgery within the existing structural frame would be required to carve out the new auditorium space.

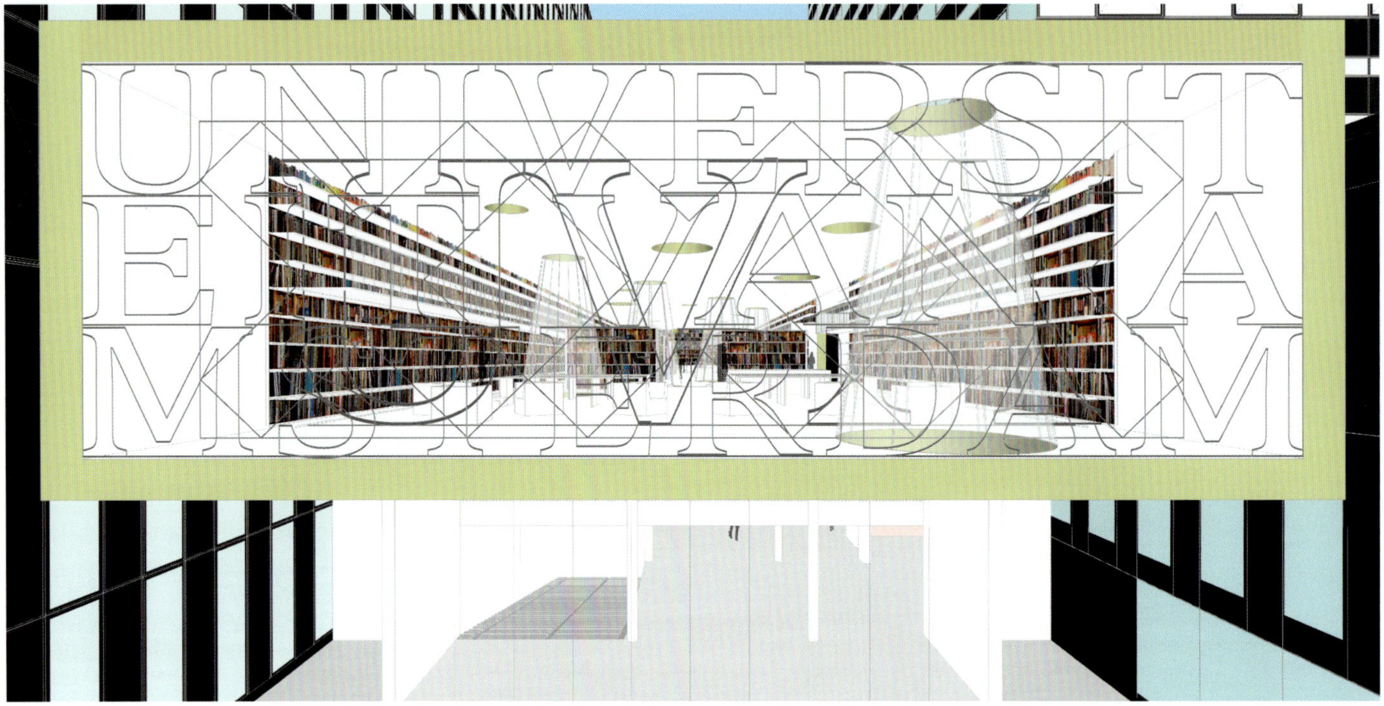

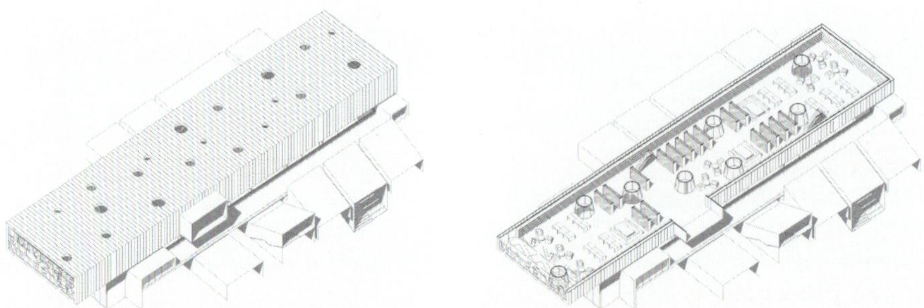

A significant brief development came when the law faculty began to explore options for building a new subject library in the upper level of the triple-height passage space. Although this option was soon rejected, the faculty's need for additional space would be addressed in later iterations of the brief.

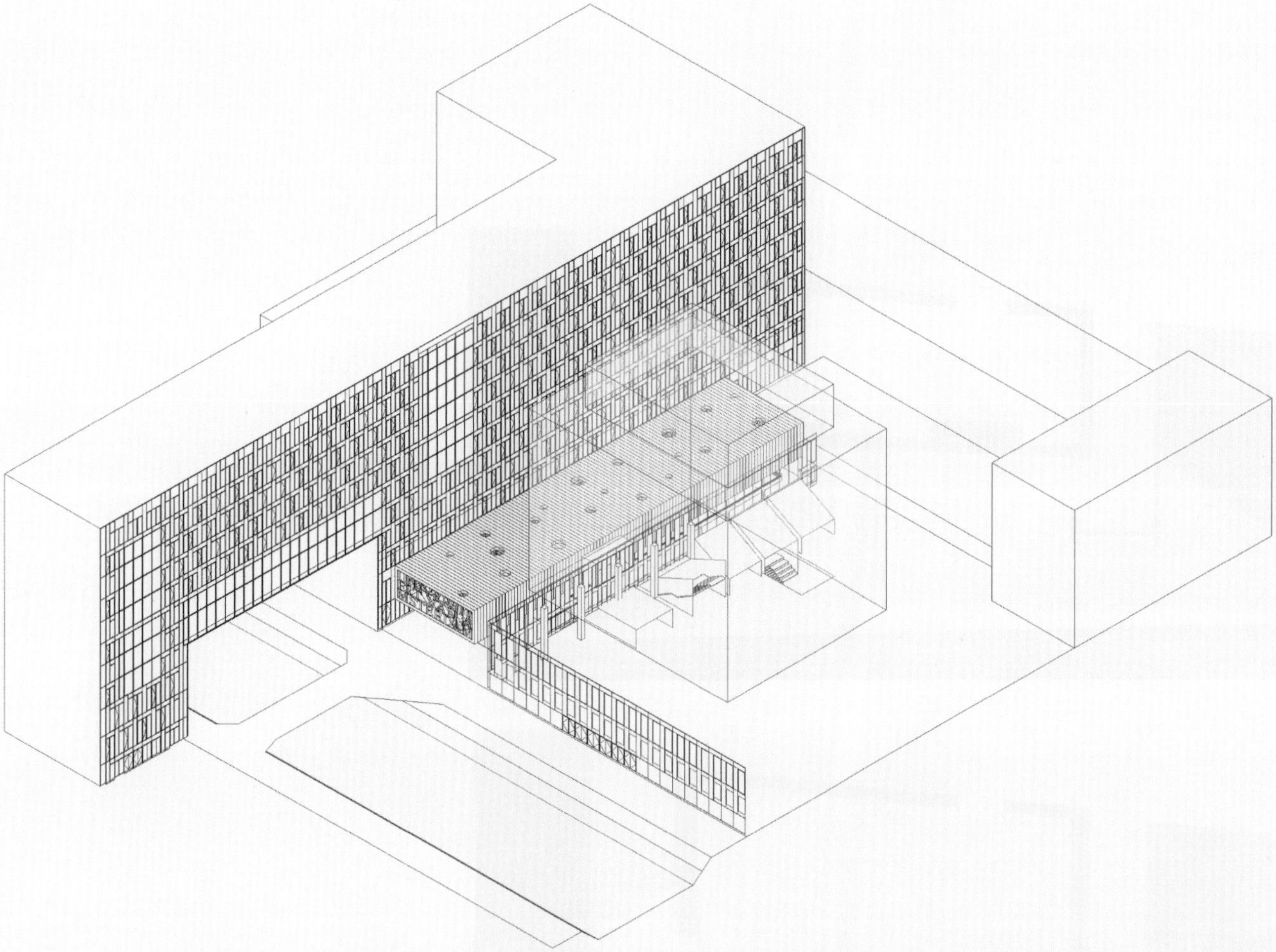

Having established that the law library would not sit at the upper levels of the passage (image above with the library, image below without), it was possible to develop the final form for the passage, and in particular its portal onto the canal.

With the law library option rejected, the interior of the passage could at last be visualised: a meeting and circulation space for the thousands of students using the Roeterseiland campus, lit by super-scaled circular rooflights. It would provide access not only to the suite of lecture rooms located in the podium, but also into the slab and tower blocks.

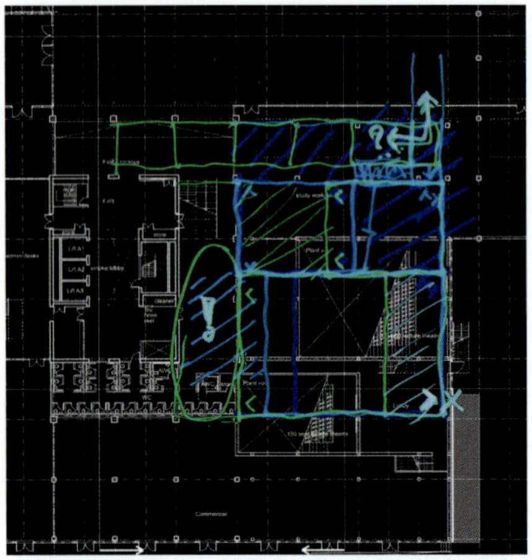

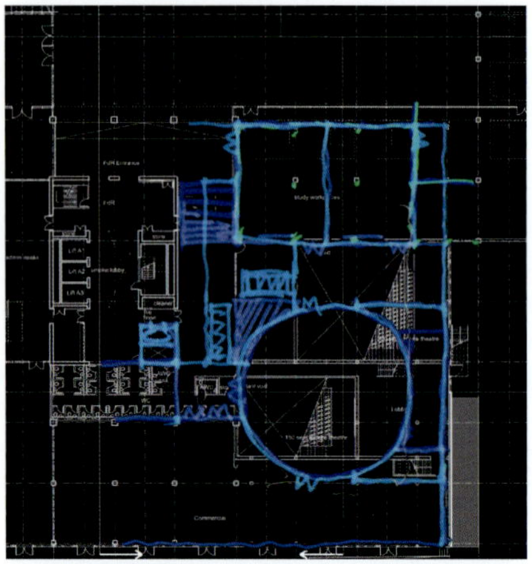

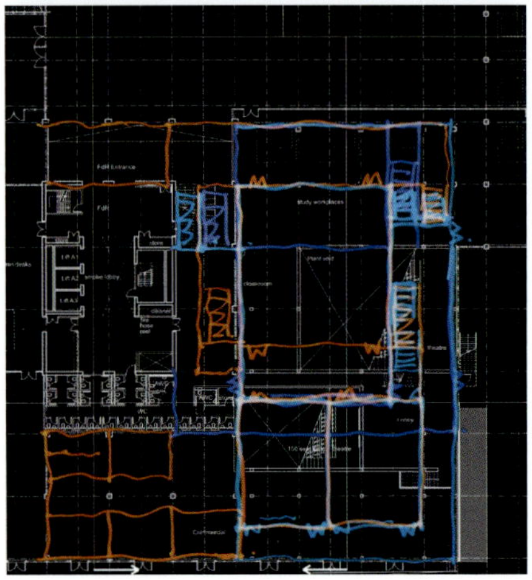

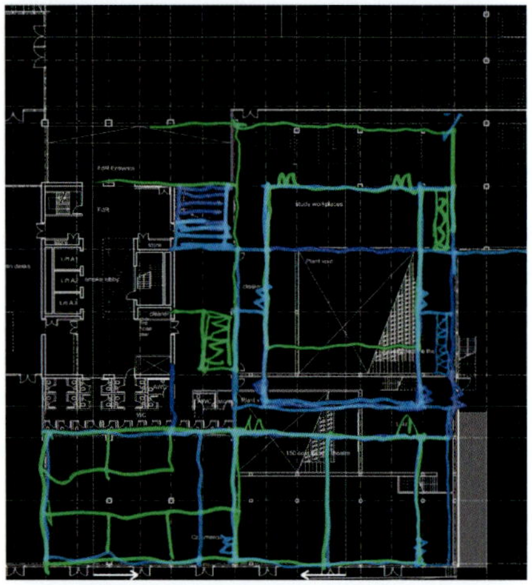

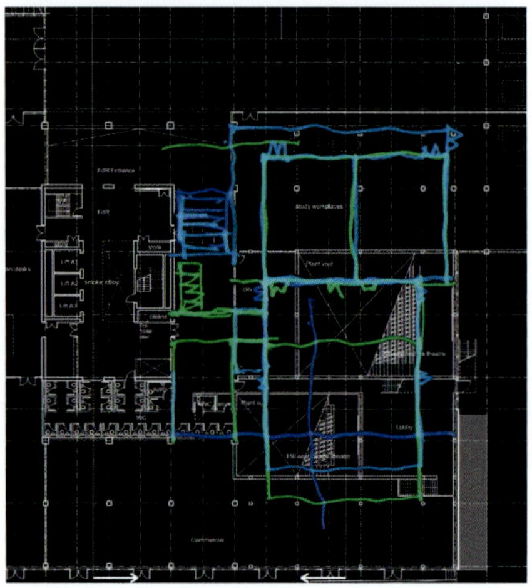

With the detailed functional brief finally established, the optimum arrangement of lecture and seminar spaces in the podium could be reached.

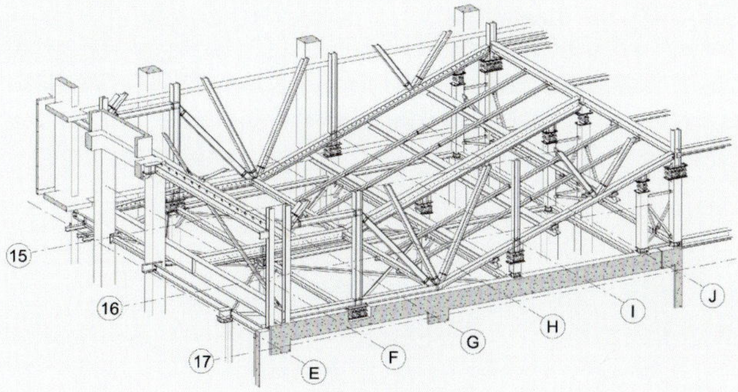

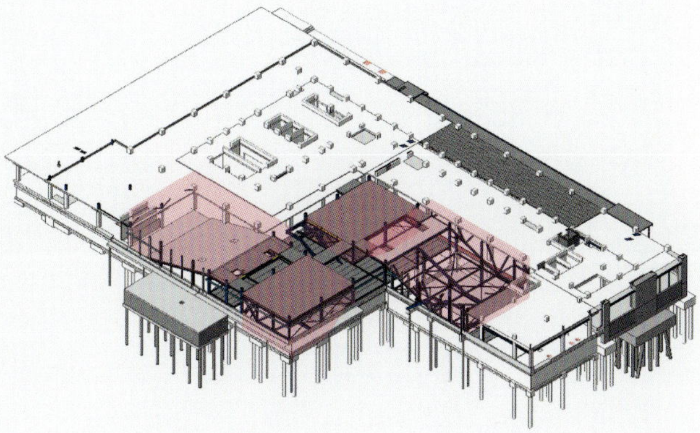

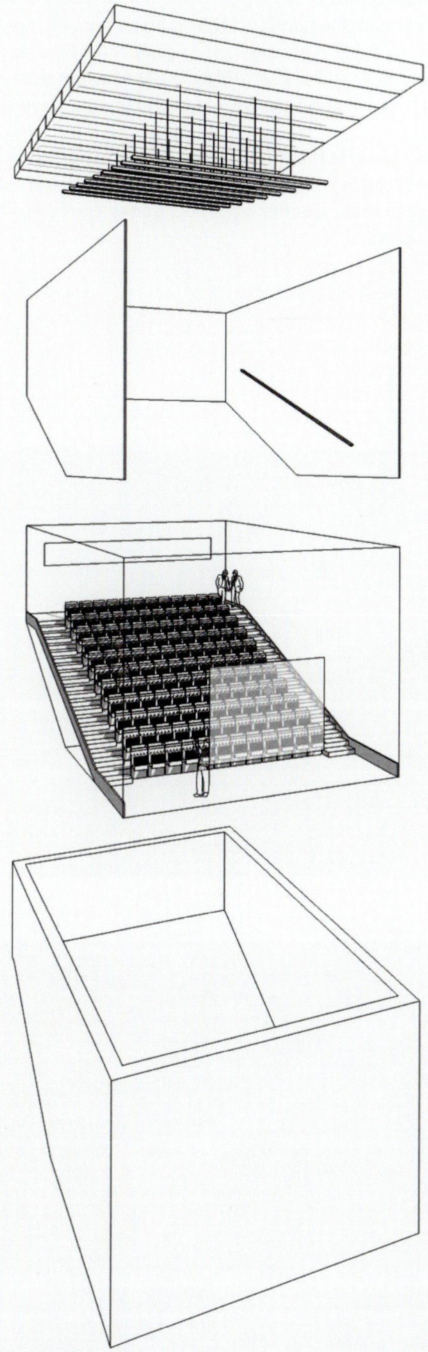

The construction and soundproofing of the auditoria spaces could also now be studied in more detail. By building them as a series of four 'boxes within a box', acoustic separation could be achieved. Each lecture-theatre volume was docked into the podium and floated on springs to minimise noise transfer.

Various options for exposing the surfaces were explored, as well as those for the acoustic 'dressing' of the internal spaces.

Journeys from the city to addresses within the campus could now be understood in more detail. A strong network of connections has been created into and across the campus (1), and an active frontage given to the podium of block A (2). An important at-grade cross-campus route is materialised in the passage and bridge (3), the former working at several levels (4), and including a lower-ground floor bicycle store. The route accesses slab block cores D (5), C (6) and B (7), as well as core A (8) into the tower. Lecture theatres are placed in the podia of buildings BC (9) and A (10), and accessed from the passage and first-floor connections. These first-floor links create a pedestrian 'circuit' (11) above the passage itself.

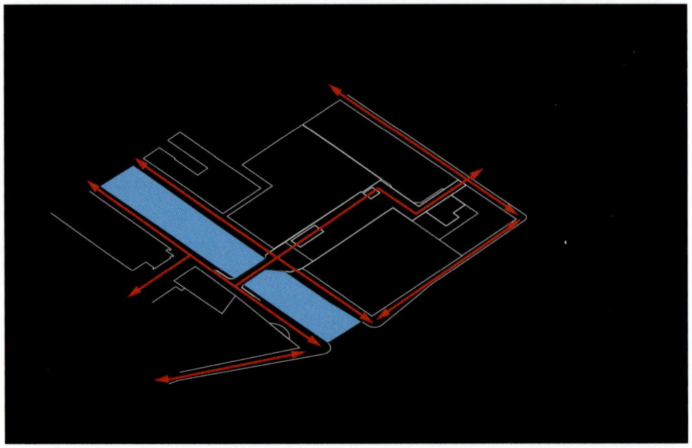

1

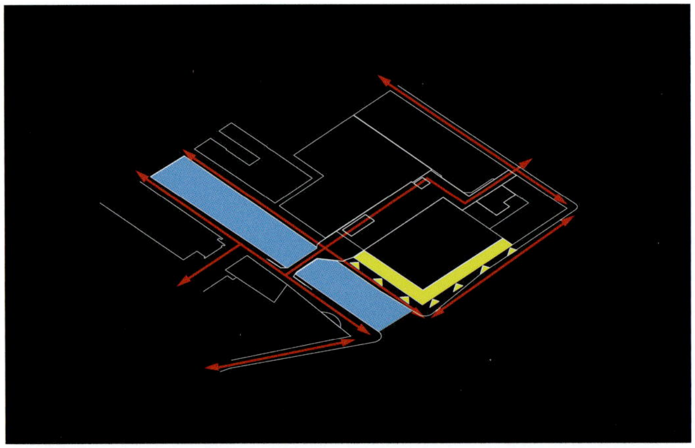

2

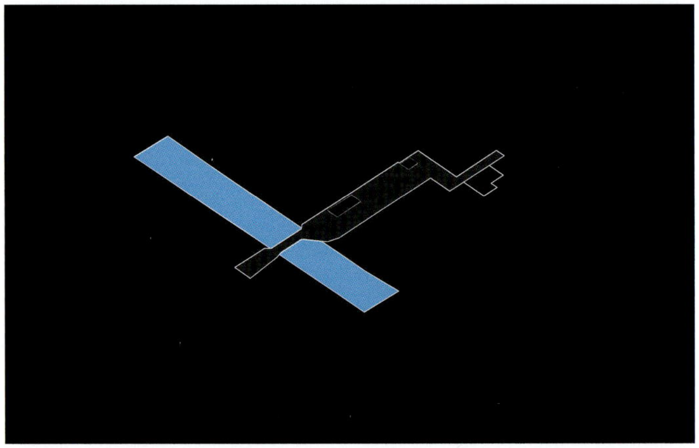

3

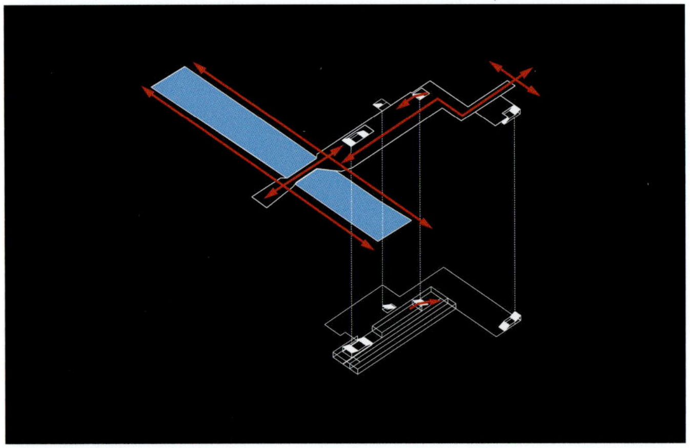

4

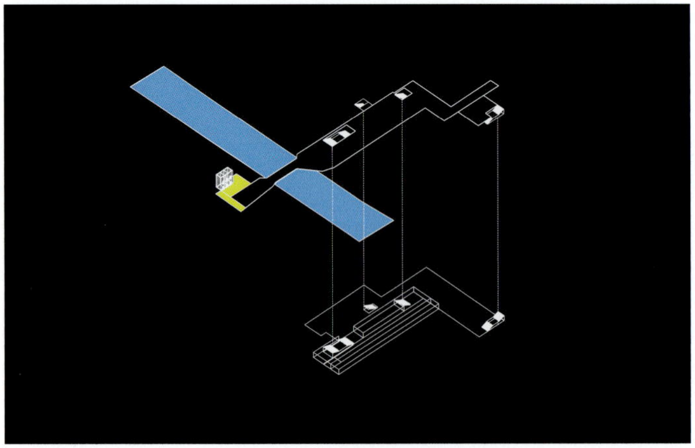

5

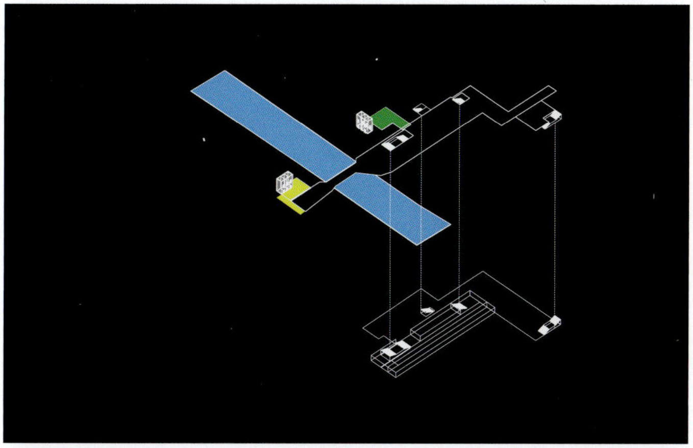
6

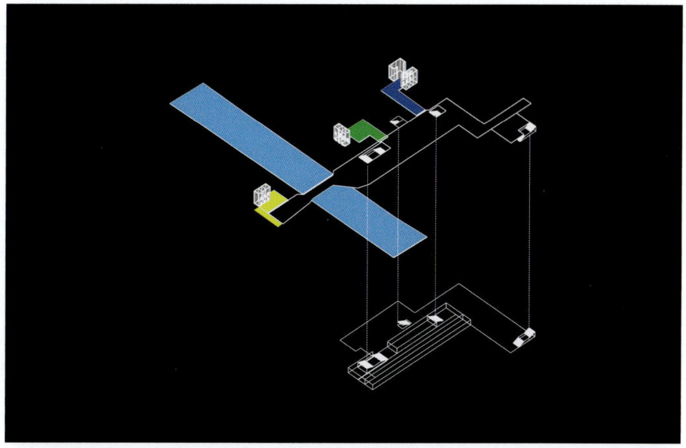
7

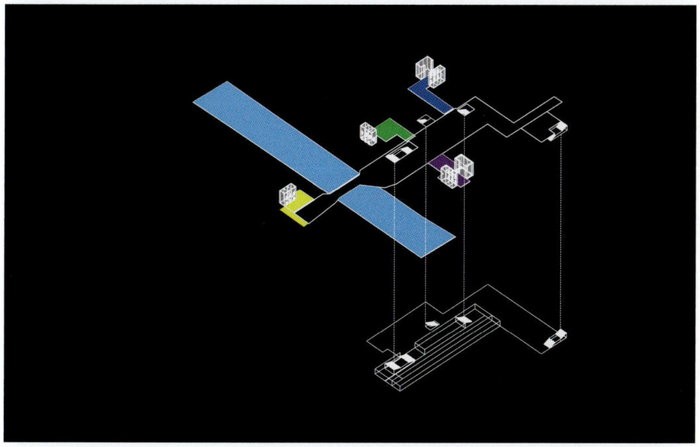
8

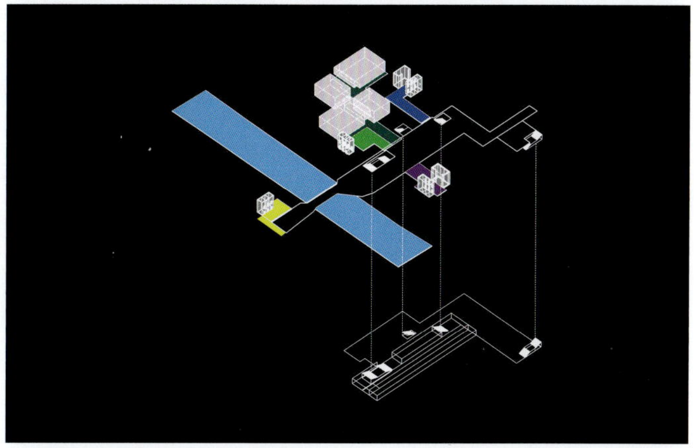
9

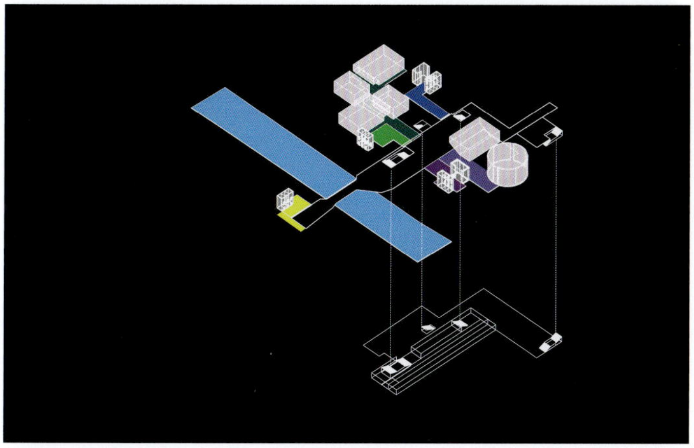
10

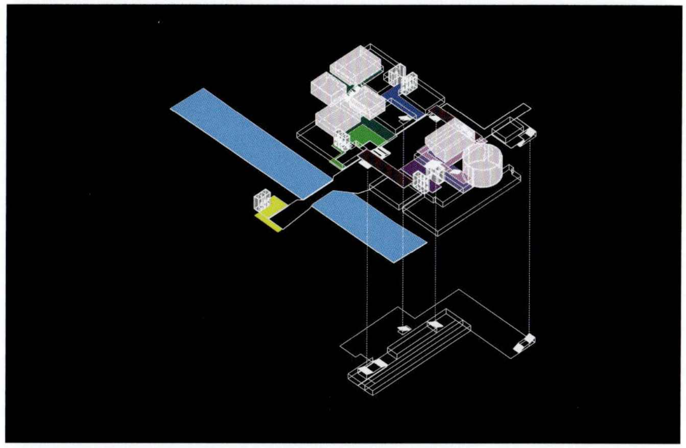
11

The idea of journeys through the building was a recurring theme as the design progressed. How would the promenade between city and lecture room look and feel? Good wayfinding and a fluid flow of spaces, both horizontal and vertical, would be essential in guiding students and staff to their destinations.

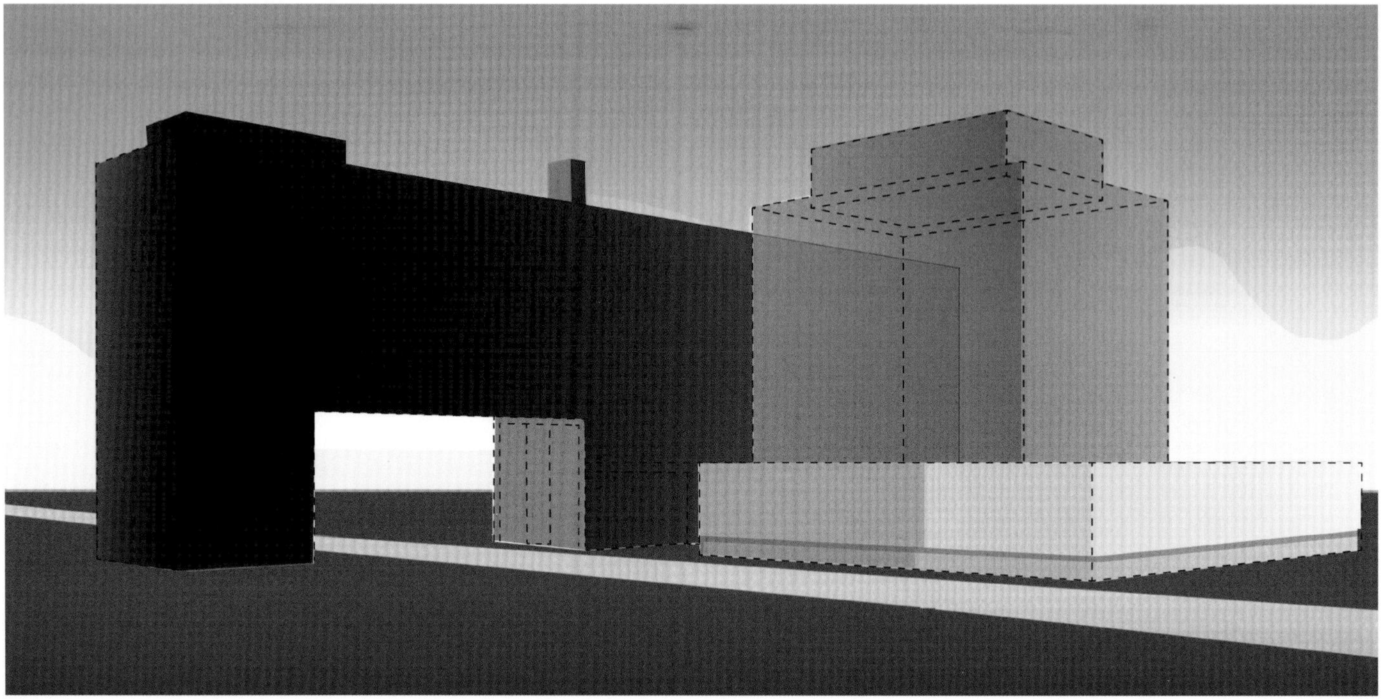

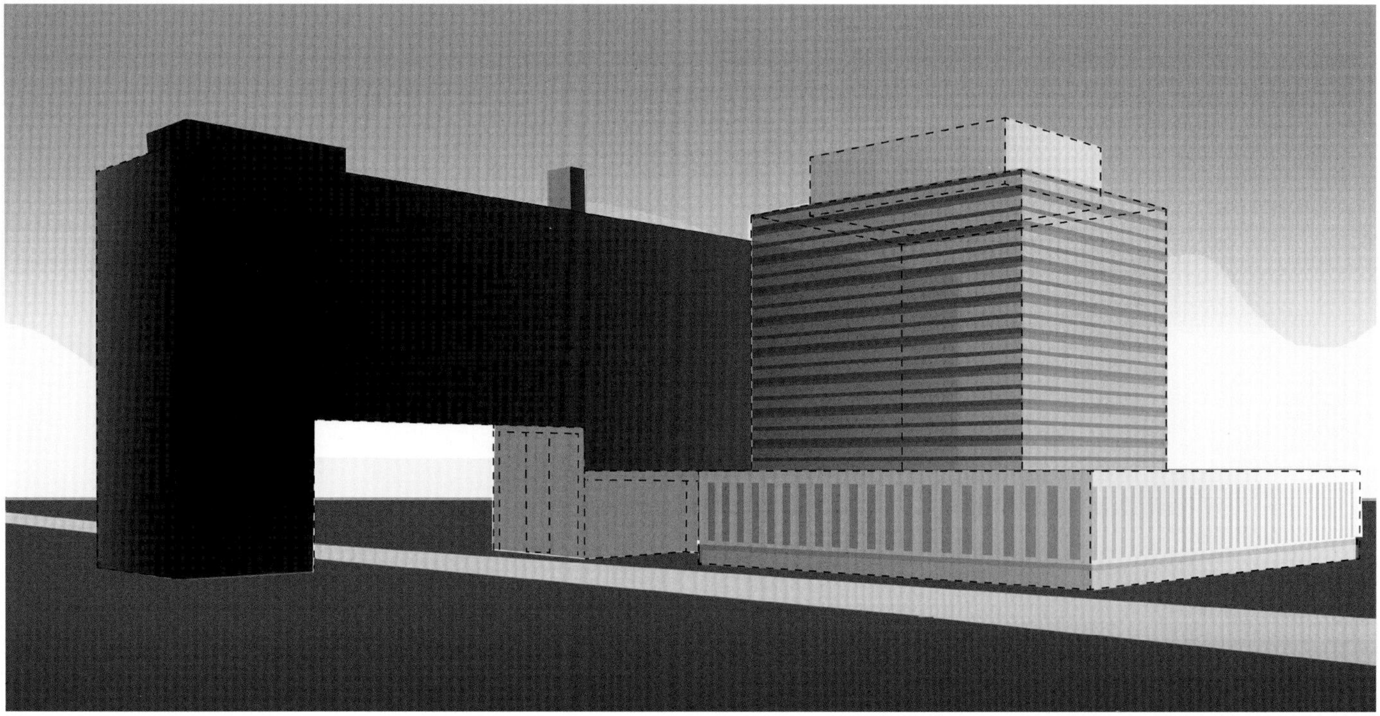

The exterior of the building was now also defined. The final ensemble would clad the two taller blocks in darker tones to give a strong silhouette against the sky, sitting them on a podium clad in lighter tones.

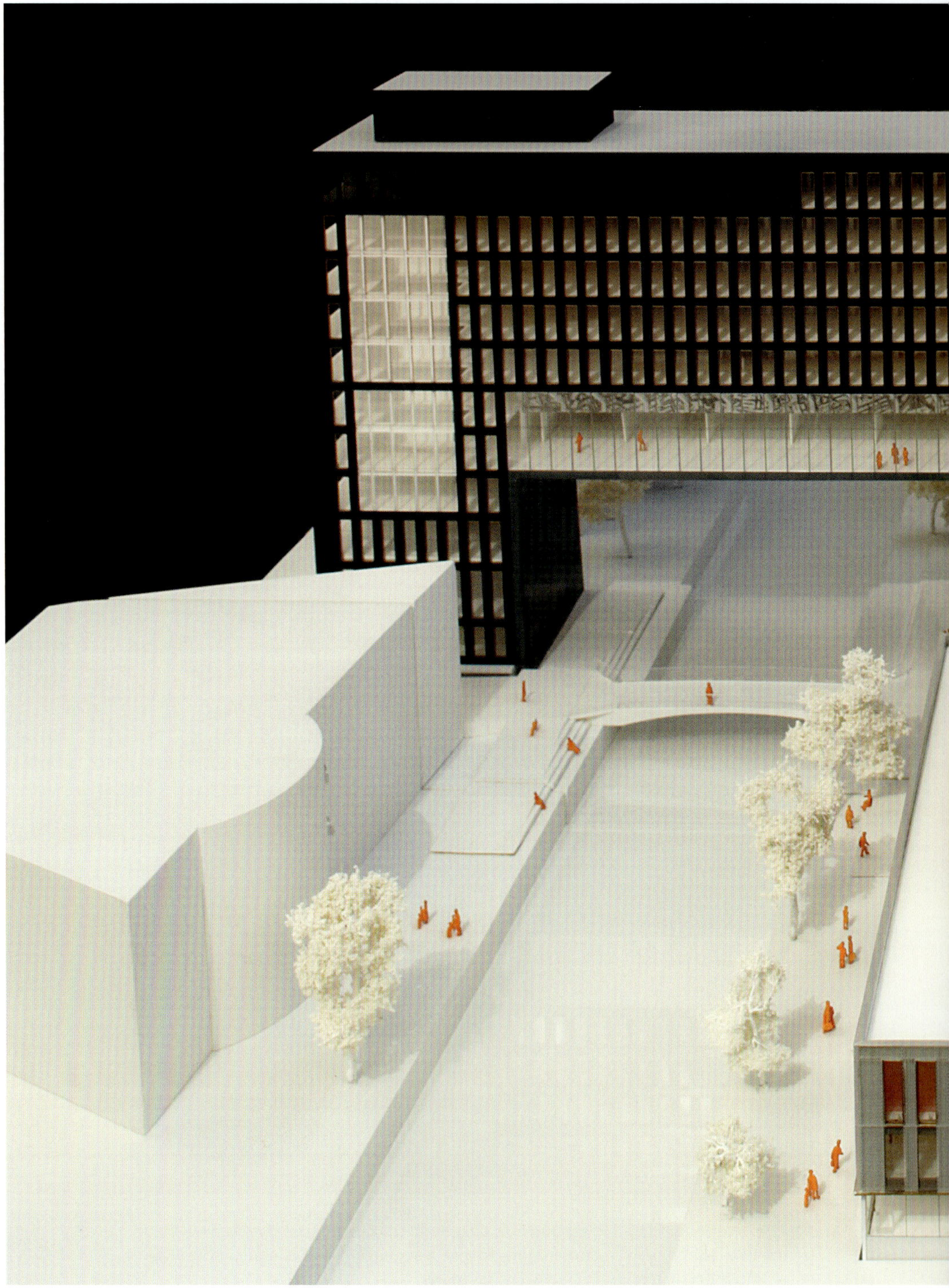

The evolving model shows the contrast between the horizontal facade treatment of the point block and the more vertical emphasis of the slab block behind.

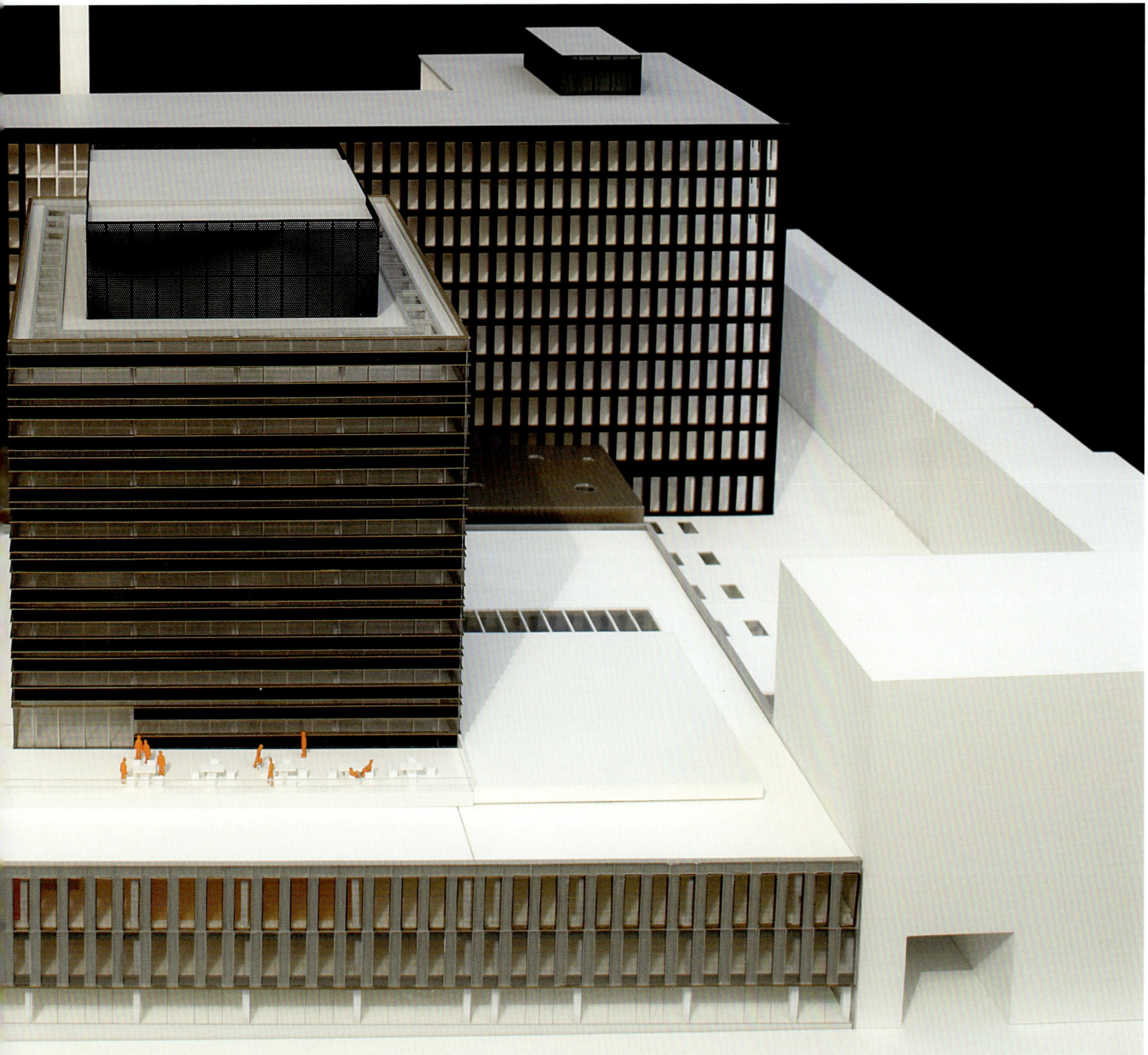

PHASE 3

AUG 09–AUG 11

IN WHICH THE FACULTY OF LAW BECOMES OUR CLIENT, WE BROADEN OUR NETWORK OF COLLABORATORS AND WE ASK HOW MANY COLOURS YOU REALLY NEED TO FIND YOUR WAY

With the main block facades now detailed, attention was turned to how they met the ground at podium level. It was already established that the main podium facade would have cladding showing a hierarchy of form, texture and detailing similar to that of the larger blocks. The eastern wall of the podium, however, would have a more modest brick treatment, elevated by adding the odd gloss-faced brick among matt ones.

The detailed design of the bridge was also complete, with a clear span of 19 metres between the springing points on either bank. The tapering steel sections from which it is constructed are 1.6 metres high at each landing, reducing at the centre to give a deck height of just 465 millimetres.

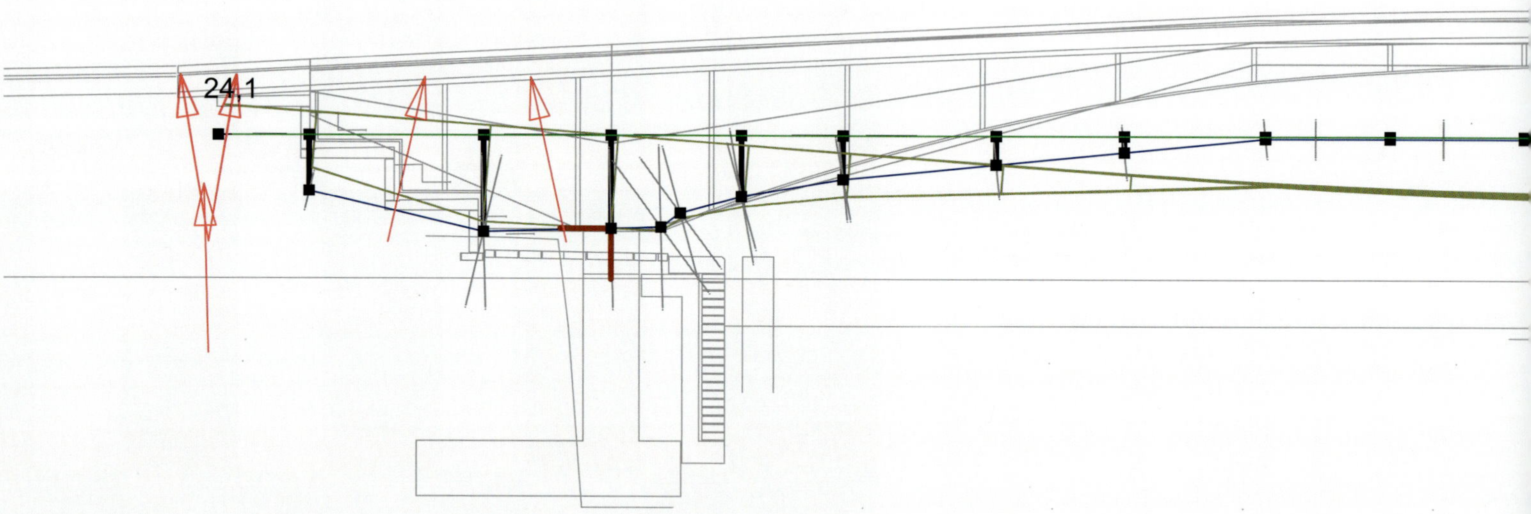

The adjacent quaysides, where the original timber piles had begun to rot away, would be rebuilt in part with sheet piles driven down in front of the existing quay. These would be hung with precast concrete panels and finished with new brickwork to restore the conventional appearance of an Amsterdam canalside.

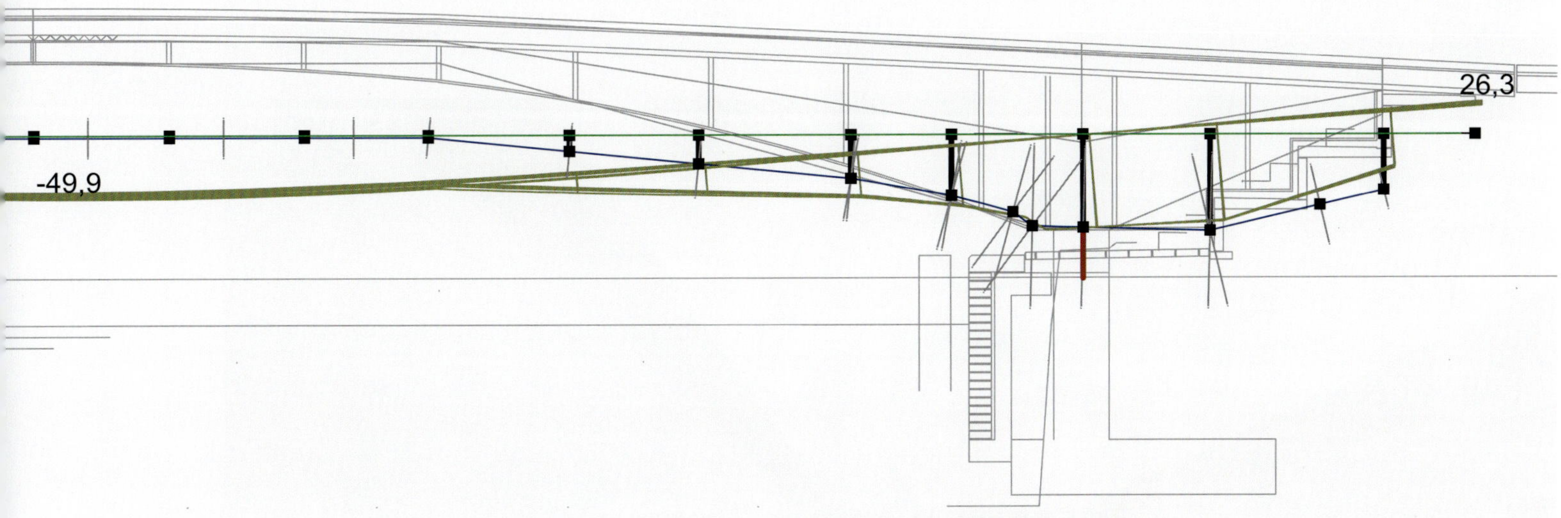

Building up on the journeys visualised through the passage and podium and up into the two blocks earlier in the process, a palette of neutral shades from white to grey was developed.

In this complex building, the monochrome background palette formed a subtle canvas for the wayfinding strategy.

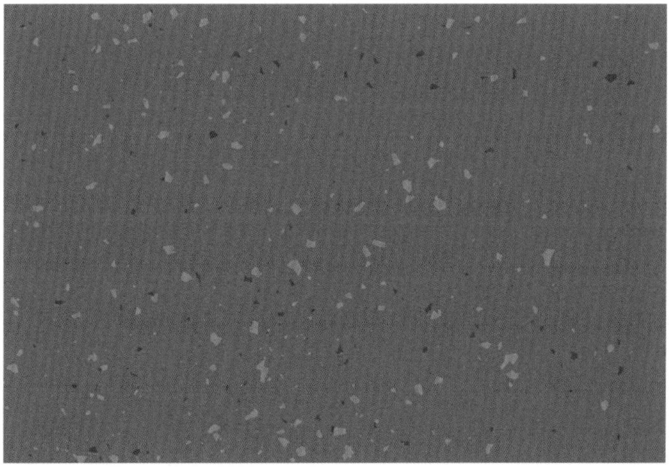

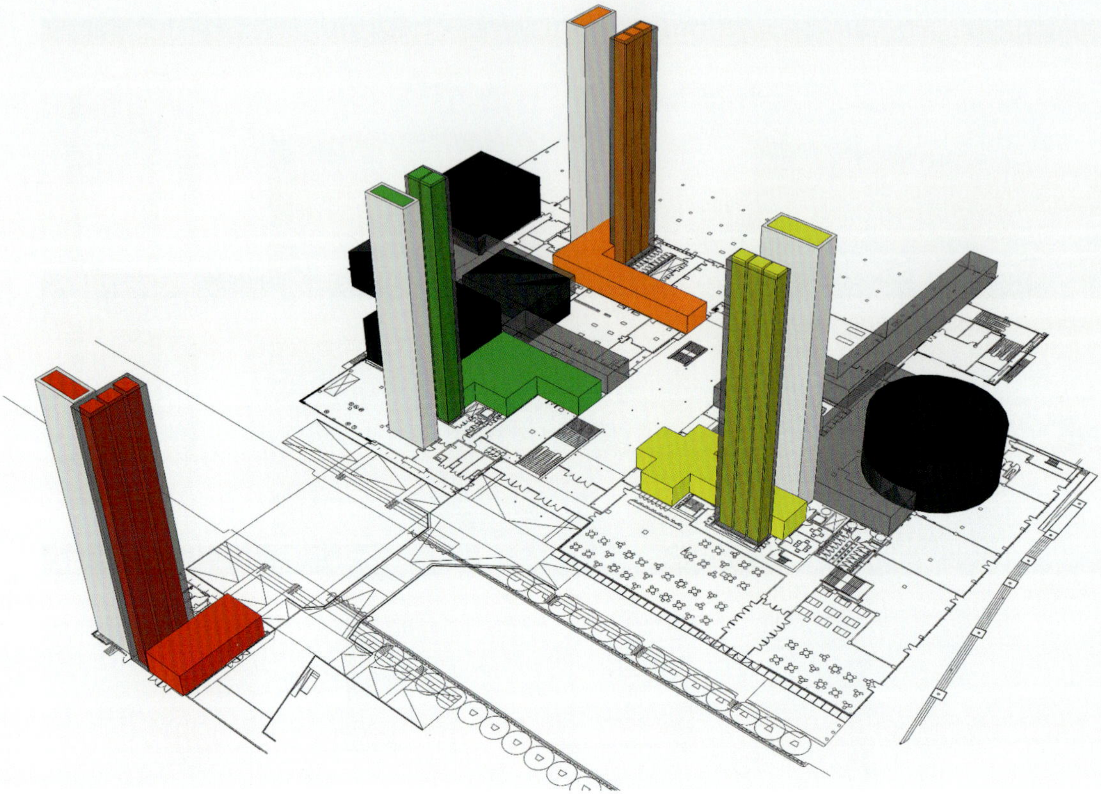

The depth and tone of the monochrome shades evolved gradually throughout the building. The volumes of the largest auditoria were signified by a deep grey, linked by landings and corridors painted in a paler tone.

The faculty 'houses' located elsewhere in the REC A and REC BC blocks, and the cores and atria leading to them, were coded with much brighter colours.

Wayfinding studies examined the visual impact of the brighter palette, looking at how the colour coding for each house would appear to users as they approached them from the passage and elsewhere in the building.

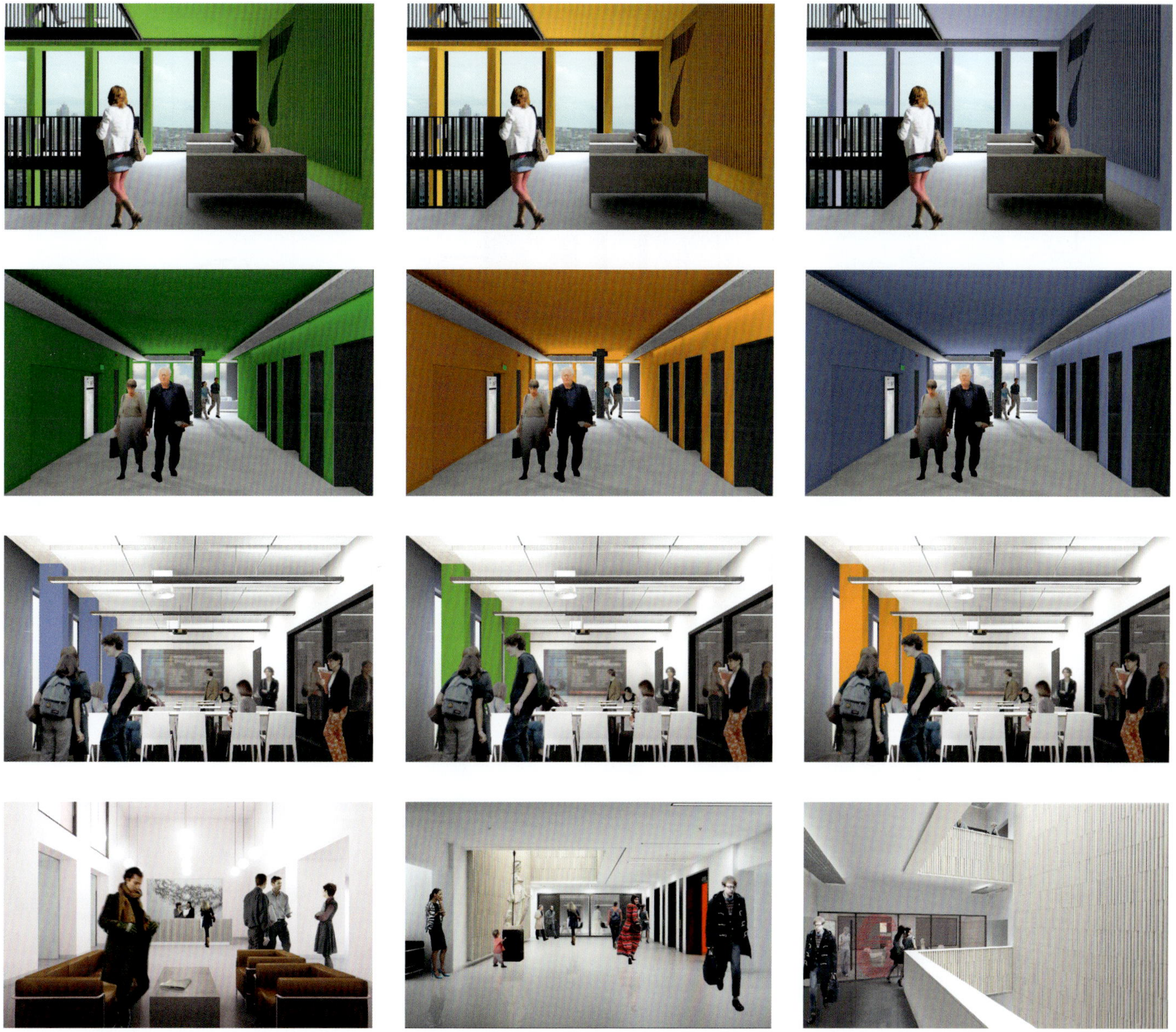

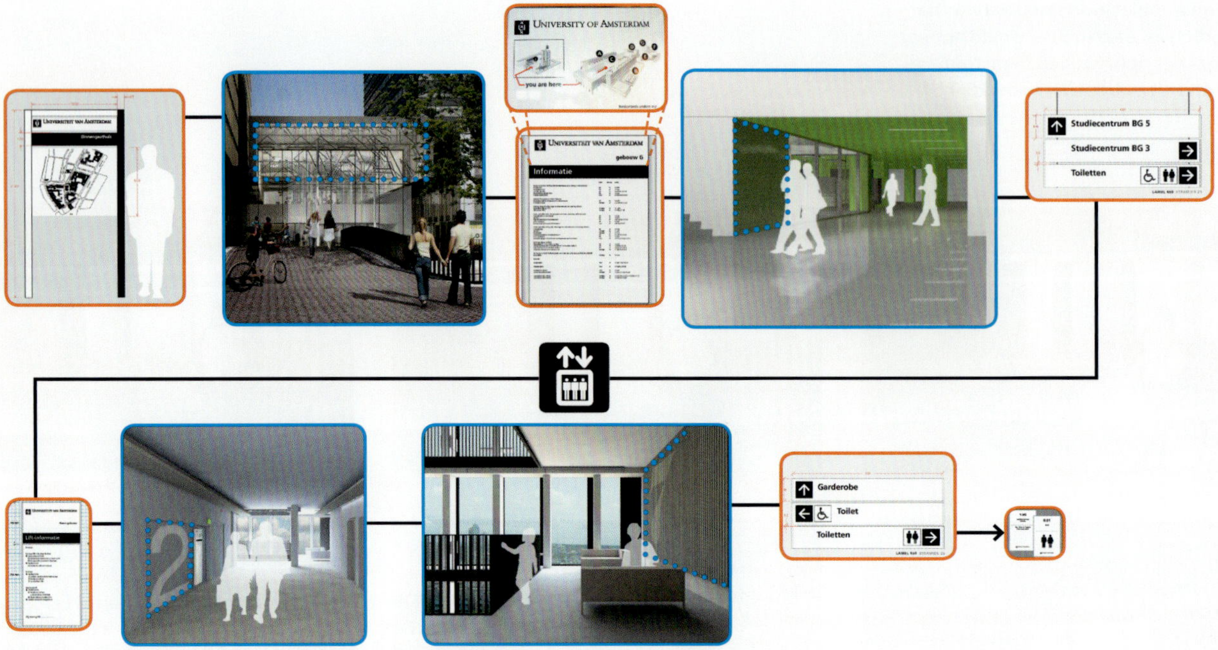
University of Amsterdam
you are here
Universiteit van Amsterdam
gebouw 6
Informatie
Studiecentrum BG 5
Studiecentrum BG 3
Toiletten
Lift-informatie
Garderobe
Toilet
Toiletten

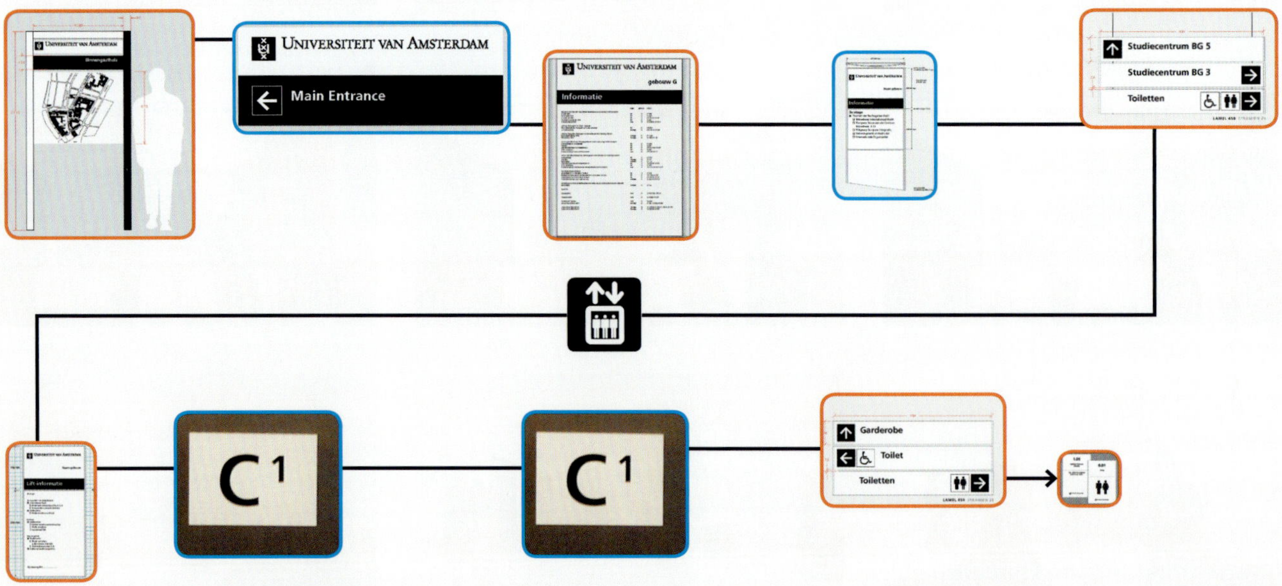
Universiteit van Amsterdam
Main Entrance
Universiteit van Amsterdam
gebouw 6
Informatie
Studiecentrum BG 5
Studiecentrum BG 3
Toiletten
Lift-informatie
C 1
C 1
Garderobe
Toilet
Toiletten

Signage was based on the university's existing system, with a hierarchy of information developed to identify more permanent, generic spaces alongside more temporary and specific ones. Areas were created to contain the multitude of self-generated signage and posters produced by each separate department.

Journeys beyond the project boundary and out into the wider campus and city were also considered, with AHMM advising on the development strategy for E Hall, immediately to the north of the canal bridge.

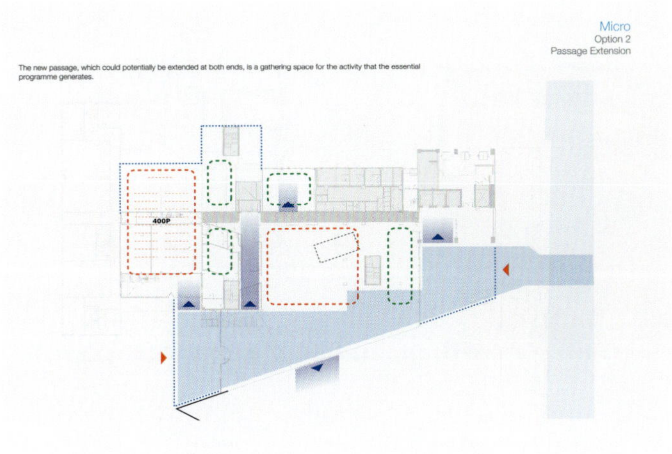

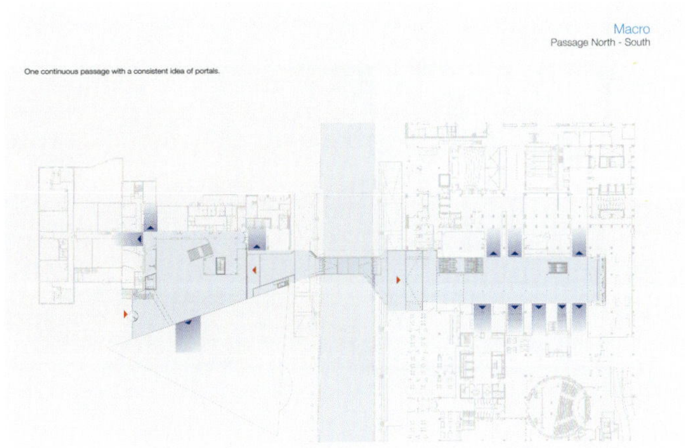

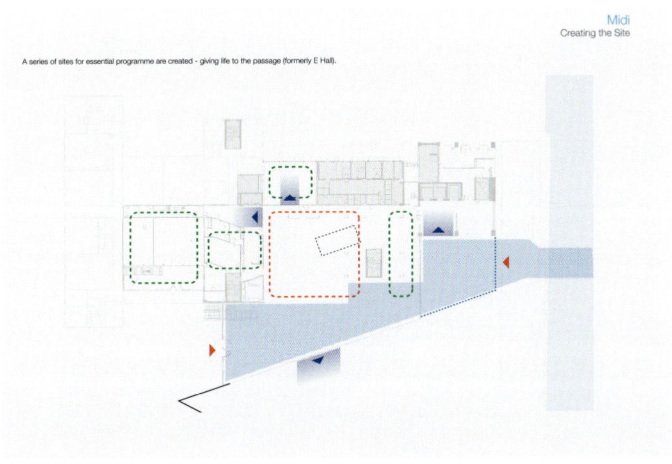

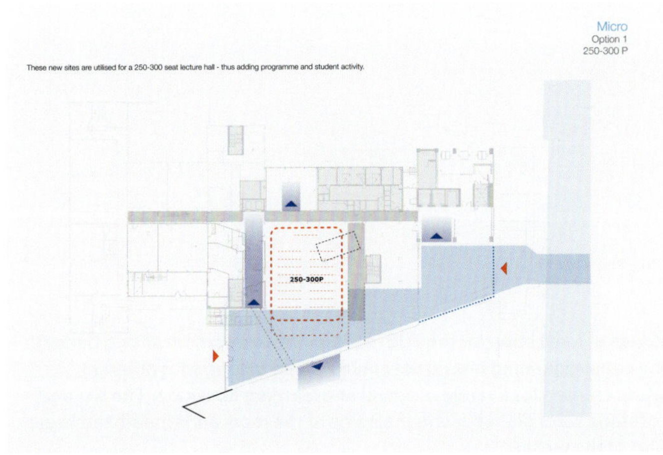

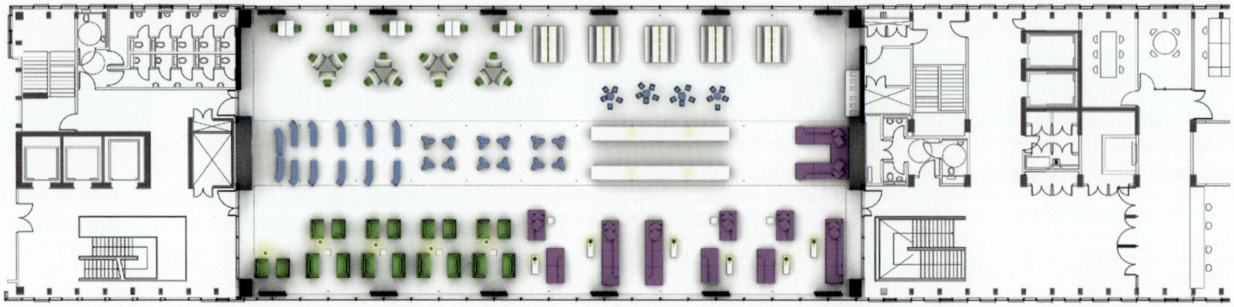

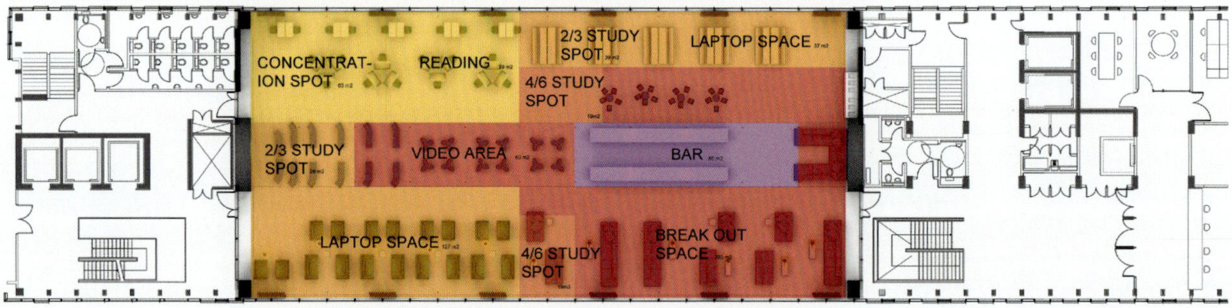

Zones of habitation for the 700-square-metre city room sitting beneath the canal-spanning box girder could now be drawn, with different areas created for a range of social and learning activities. The bar and cafeteria were placed along the spine of the room underneath the lower part of the girder.

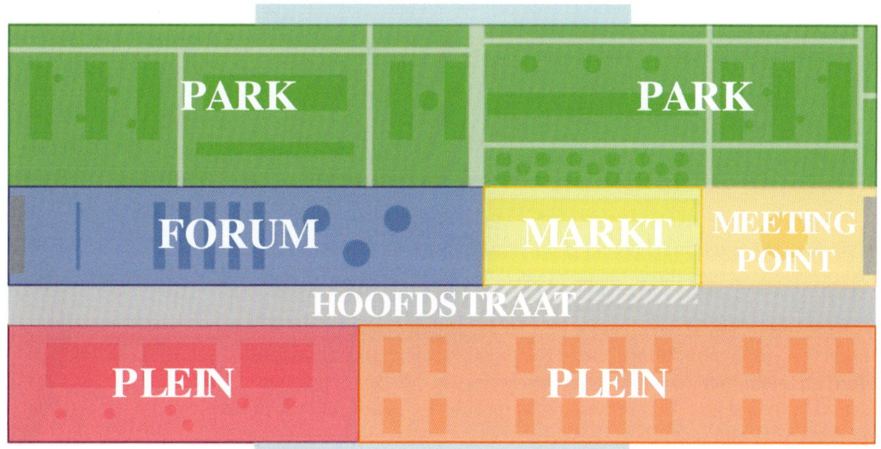

Once these zones had been established, AHMM collaborated with an interior designer on the furnishing of the city room. Several interiors specialists were involved across the two Gawronski buildings – and in particular in the design of the learning landscapes – including Fokkema & Partners and PUUR interieurarchitecten.

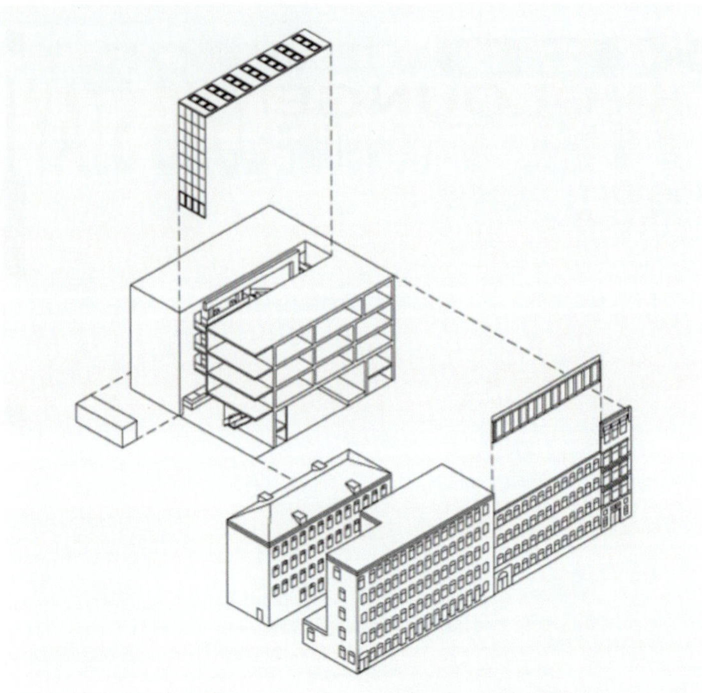

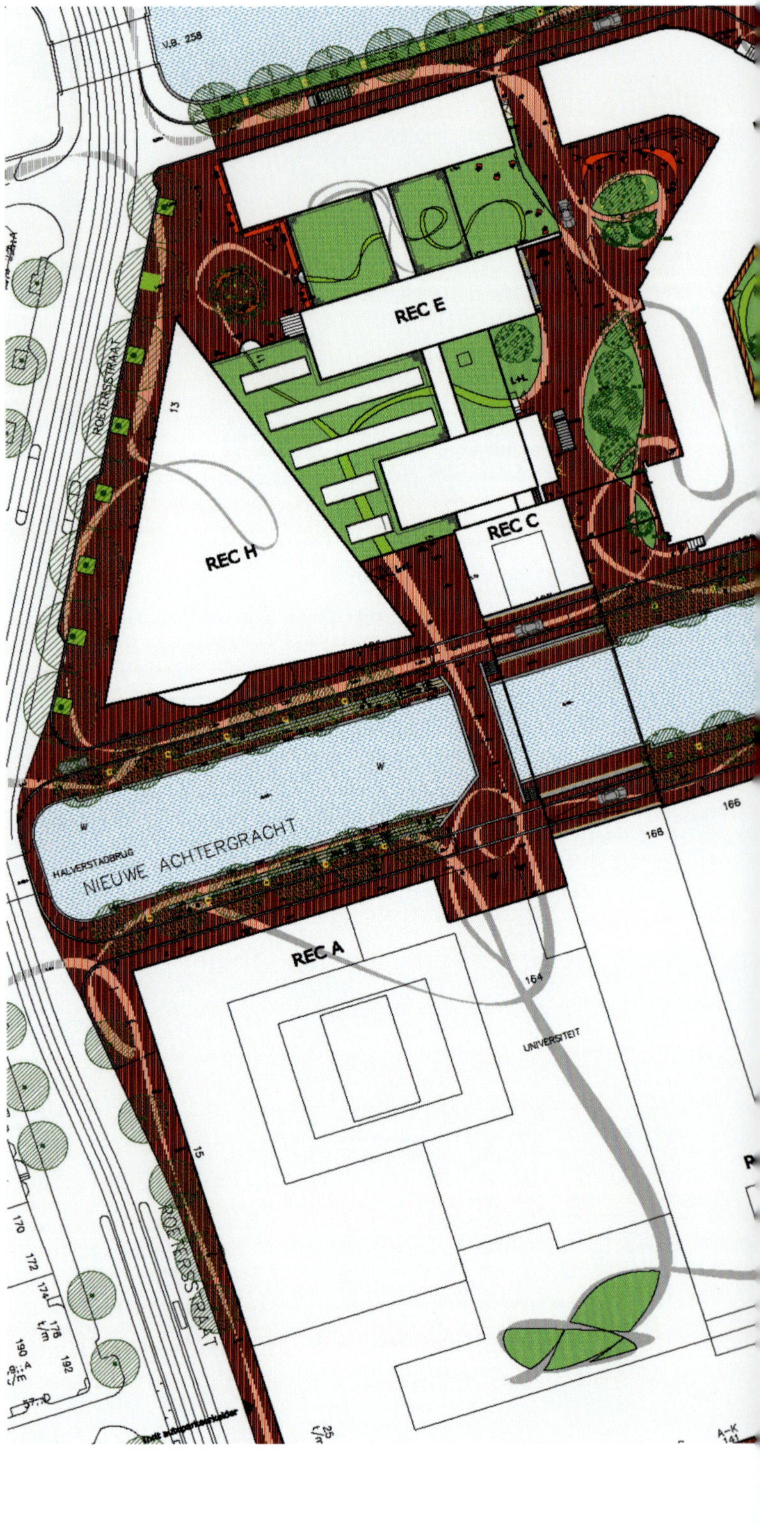

As work on the Gawronski blocks progressed, so too did AHMM's collaborations across the wider campus.

With the relocation of the university's CREA cultural centre to Roeterseiland, Simon Allford joined the panel to select an architect to refurbish the former diamond-polishing factory to the east of the site. Joost Glissenaar and Architecten van Mourik were chosen, and the project completed in autumn 2015.

Simon also joined the selection panel for a landscape architect to create a framework for the outdoor space at Roeterseiland. Inside Outside's design helps to connect the many different buildings – including the Gawronski blocks and the new CREA – using white marker stones in red paving as a subtle guide to navigation.

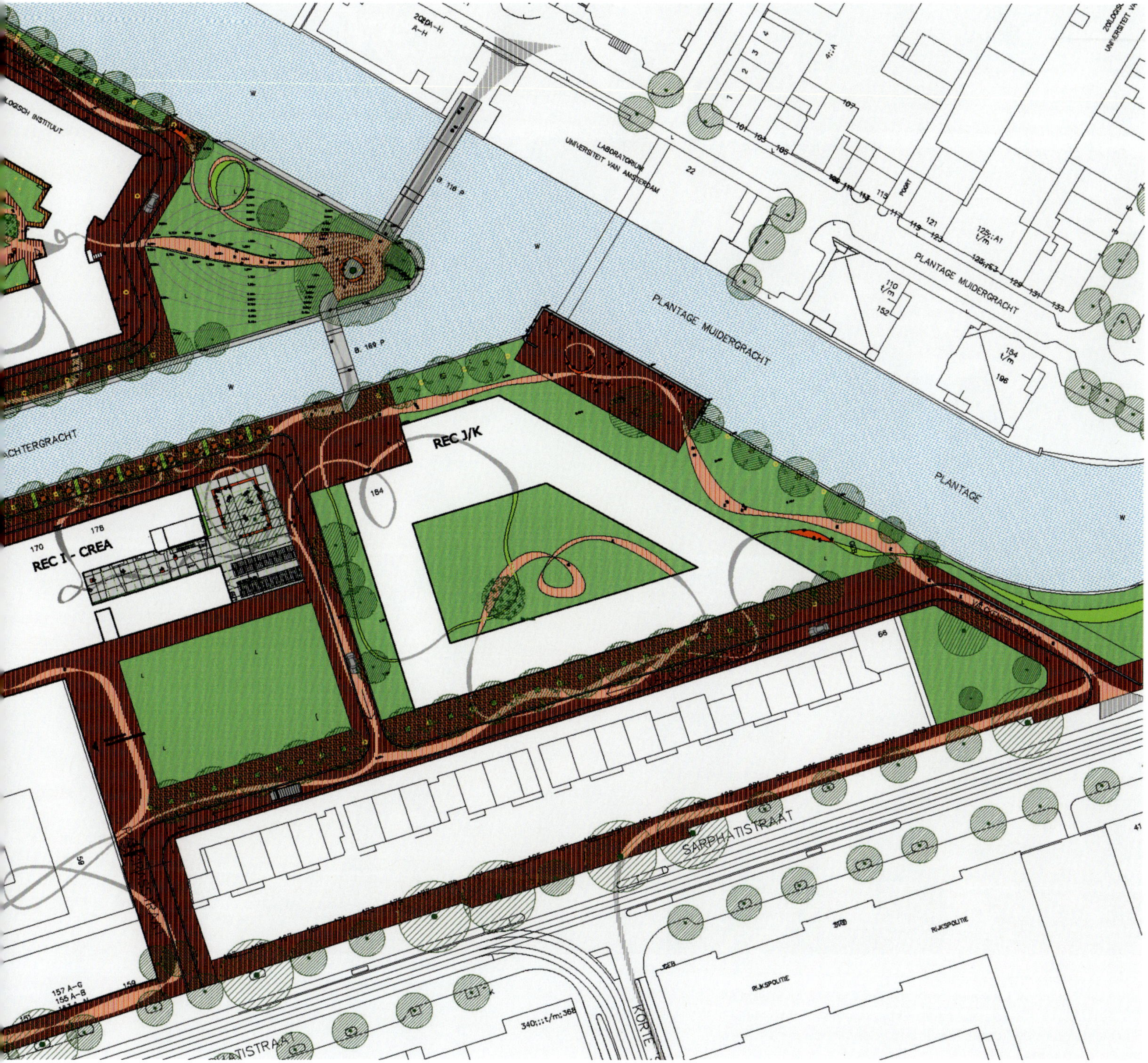
PLANTAGE MUIDERGRACHT
LABORATORIUM UNIVERSITEIT VAN AMSTERDAM
PLANTAGE
REC J/K
REC I - CREA
SARPHATISTRAAT
RIJKSPOLITIE

With the Faculty of Law now confirmed as the new occupant of the point block, the spaces inside were planned in more detail. These include a dedicated law library, roof terrace and a suite of moot courtrooms.

The Amsterdam artist Barbara Broekman was appointed to create several large-scale artworks within the space so that it had a similar 'house' feeling to the departments located in the slab block. The seven-storey-deep atrium is 'wallpapered' with a huge piece, 30 metres high by 4.5 metres wide, which is entitled *Justice and Injustice*. A second work for the faculty, *Lady Justice*, again collages images from the arts and popular culture.

September 2007 October 2007 November 2007 April 2008

As work progressed towards construction, the final iterations of plan and section were consolidated.

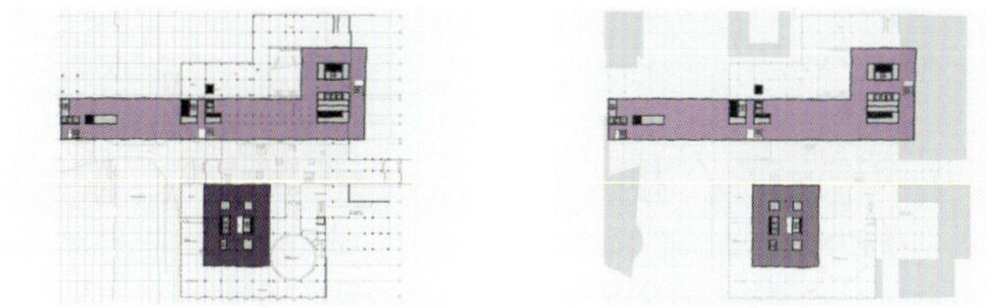

May 2008

February 2009

September 2010

The vast number and variety of room types could also be seen for the first time, from cell-like, single-occupancy offices, through shared departmental spaces, seminar and lecture rooms, to the huge city room, passage and bridge spaces capable of accommodating thousands of students.

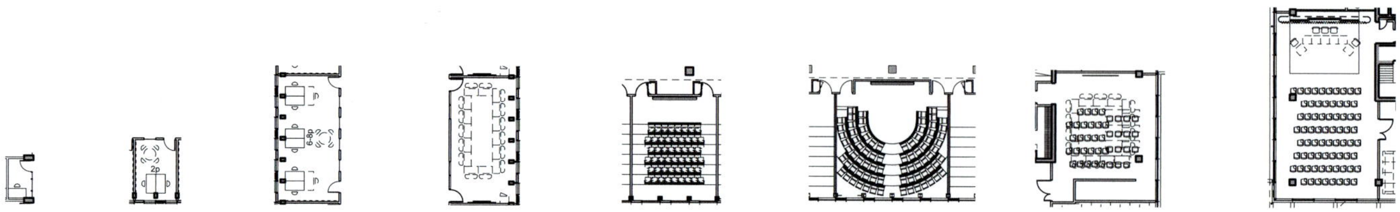

1-2 people
196 no.

8 people
62 no.

30 people
57 no.

60 people
3 no.

80 people
3 no.

50 people
1 no.

100 people
1 no.

Working

Learning

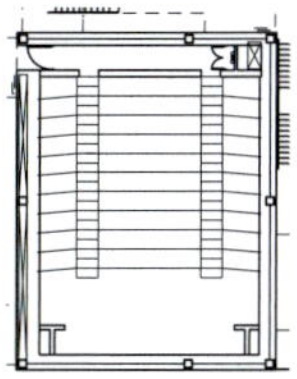

150 people
4 no.

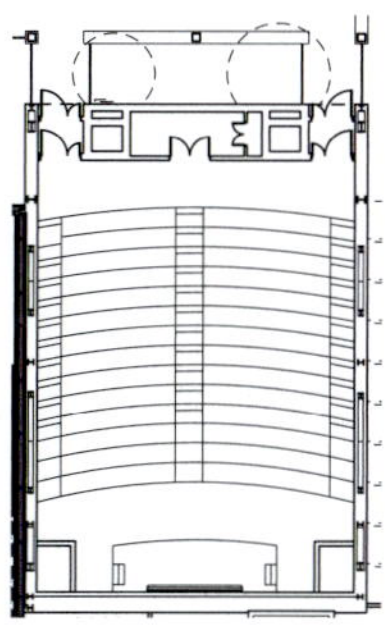

300 people
2 no.

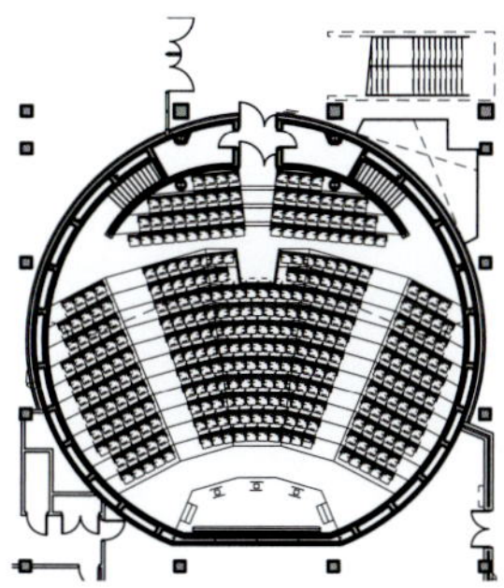

450 people
1 no.

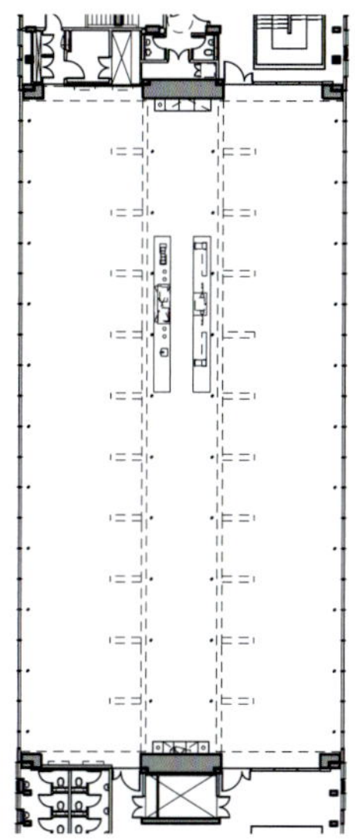

200 people
1 no.

Socialising

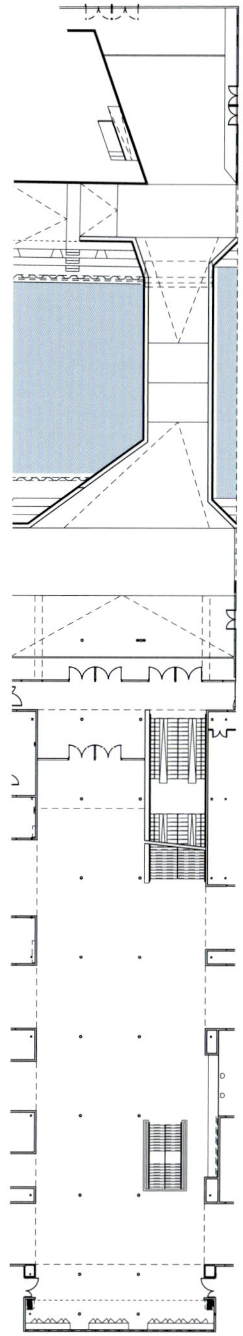

2000 people
1 no.

Circulating

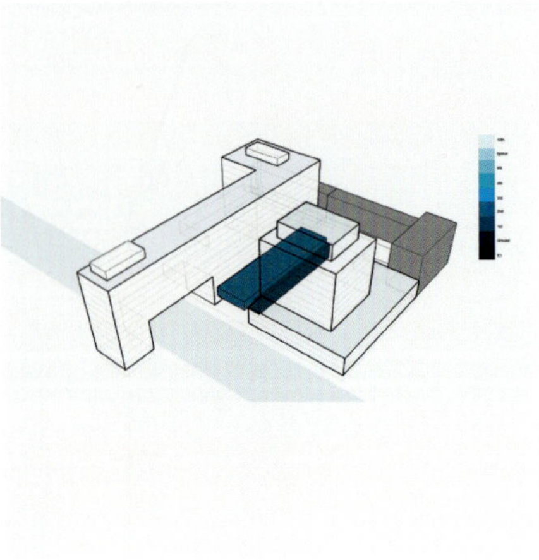

Passage

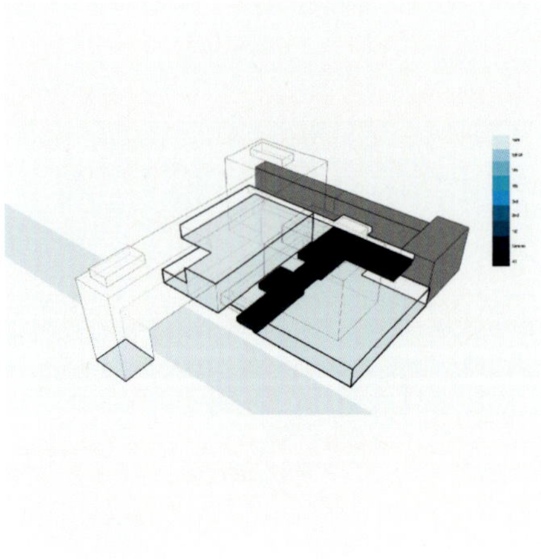

Cycle parking

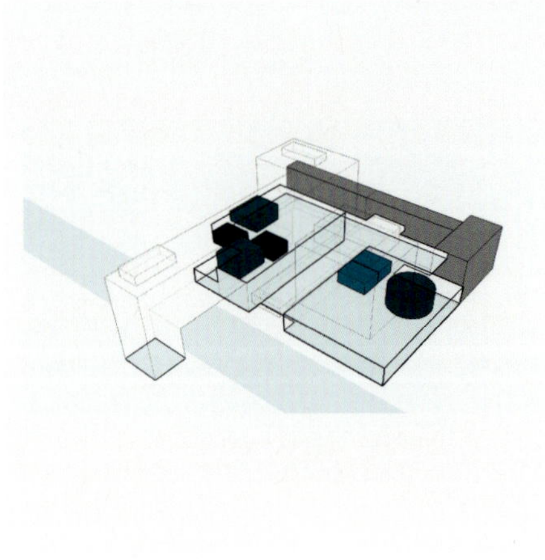

Lecture rooms

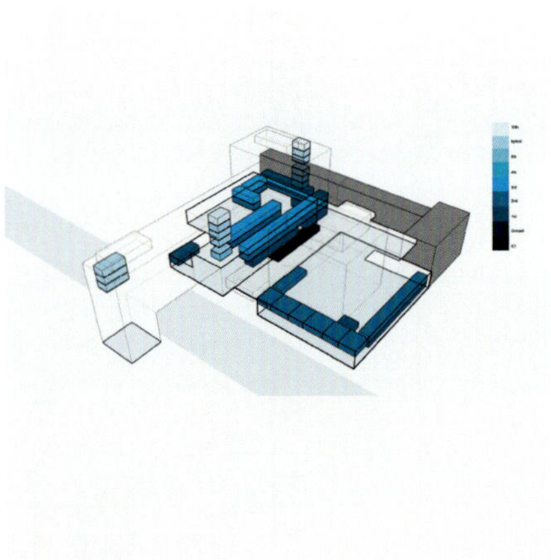

Tutorial rooms

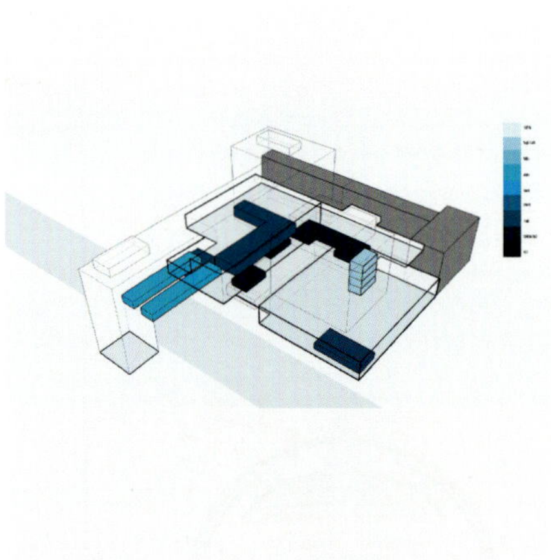

Study landscapes

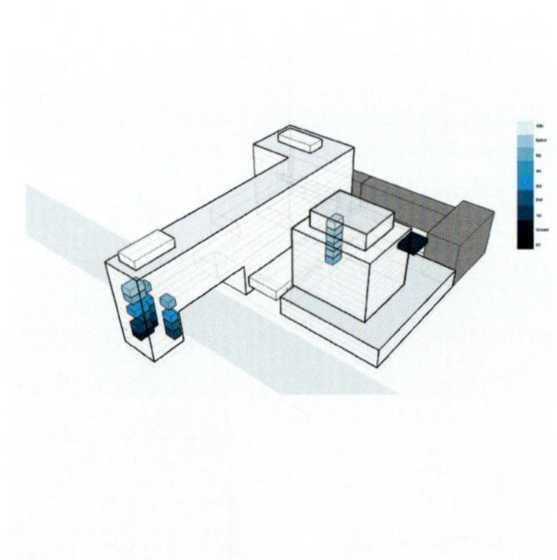

Student societies

Routes through the building were now set out as a memorable promenade, with people movement guided by clear wayfinding to a set of specific addresses. These patterns of movement help to promote interaction but also establish new pedestrian routes to the lower floors of each building, to avoid putting too much strain on the existing lift cores.

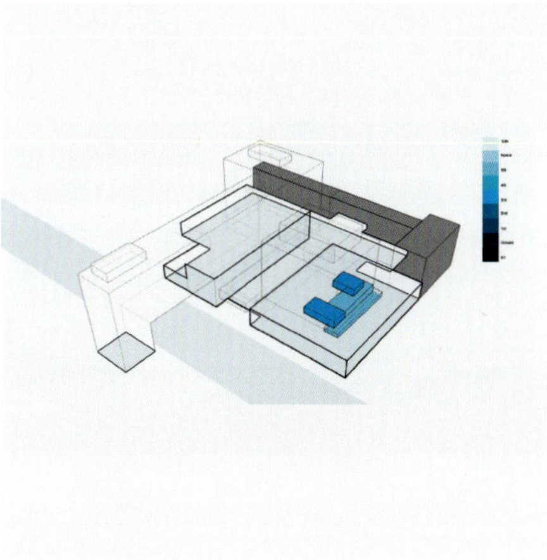

Moot court

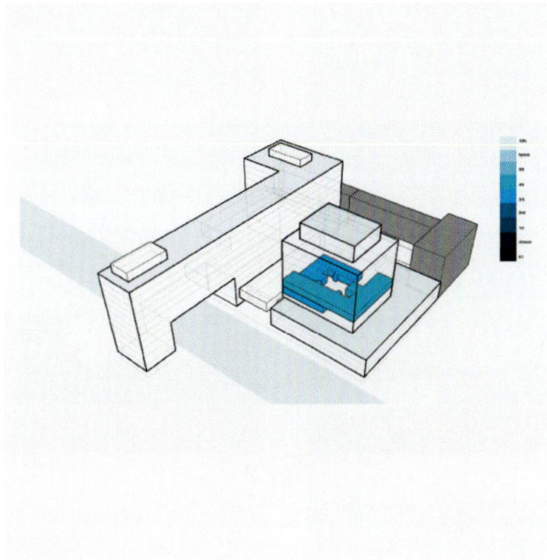

Library

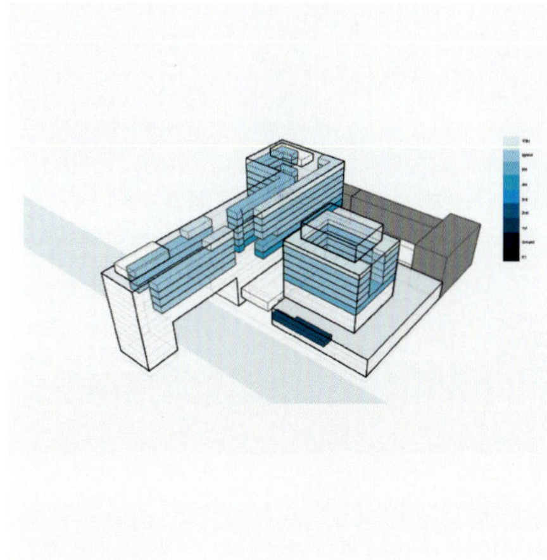

Staff offices

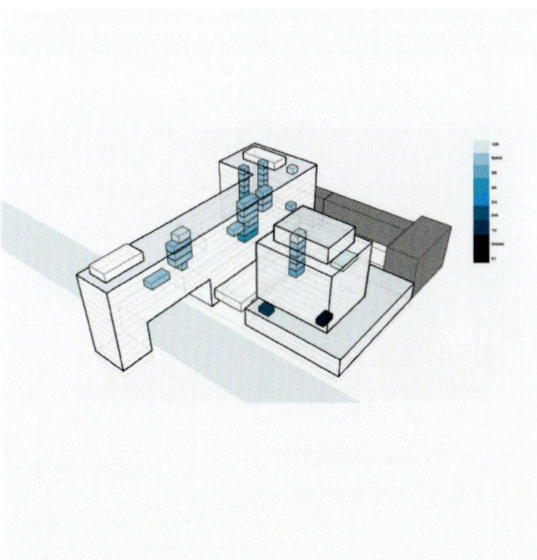

Meeting and quiet rooms

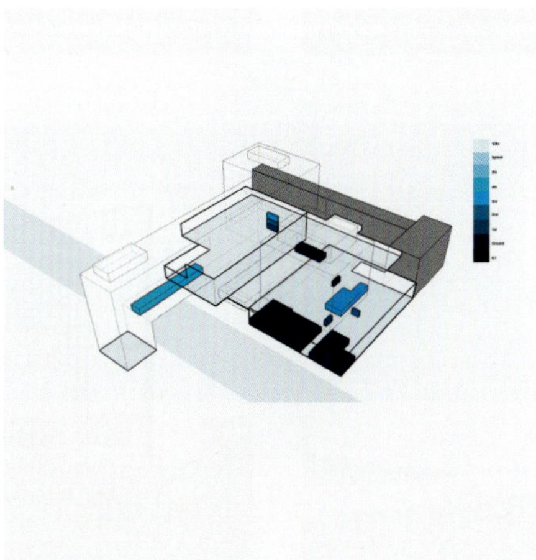

Catering

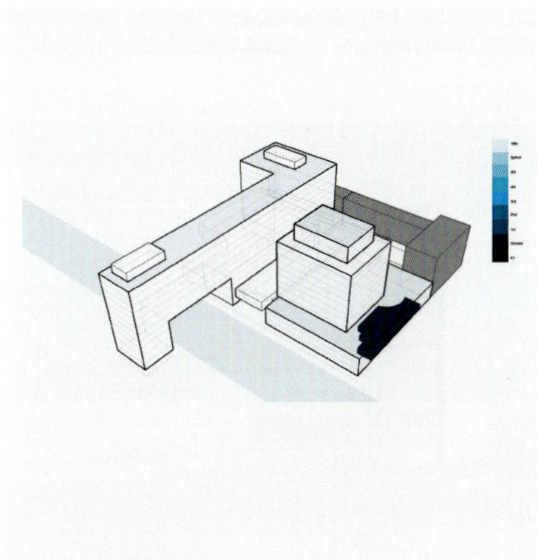

Commercial units

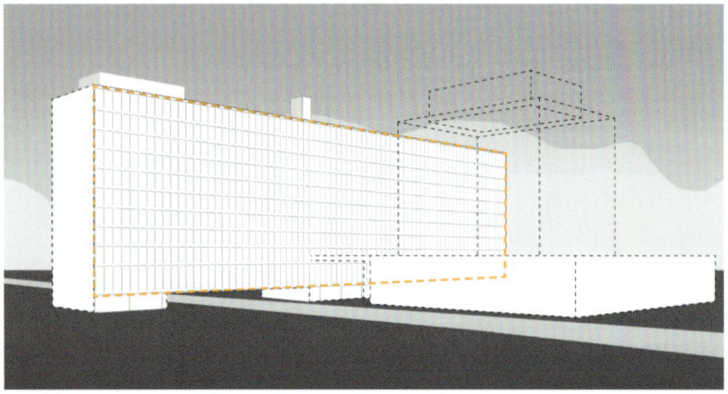

1

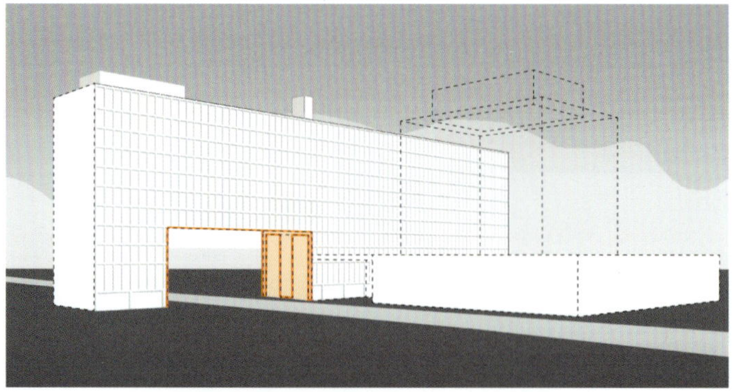

2

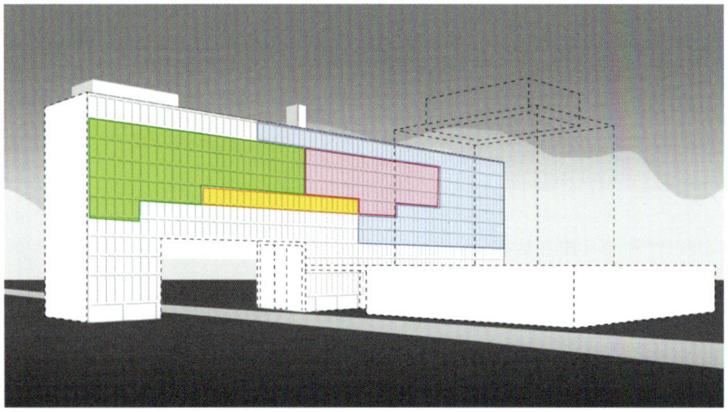

3

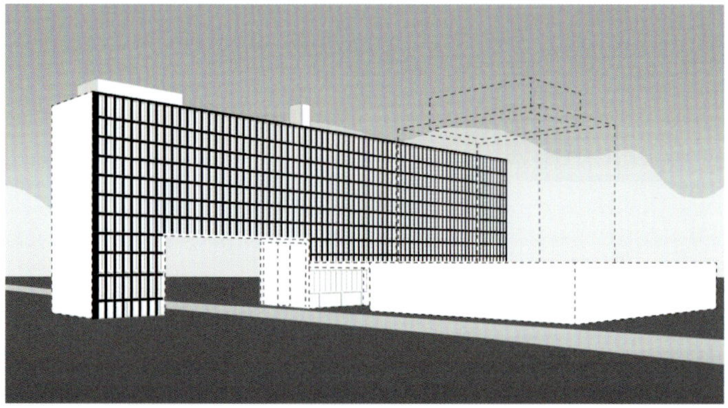

4

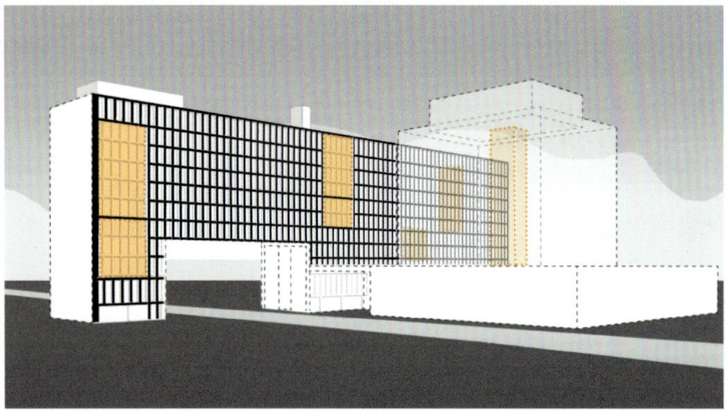

5

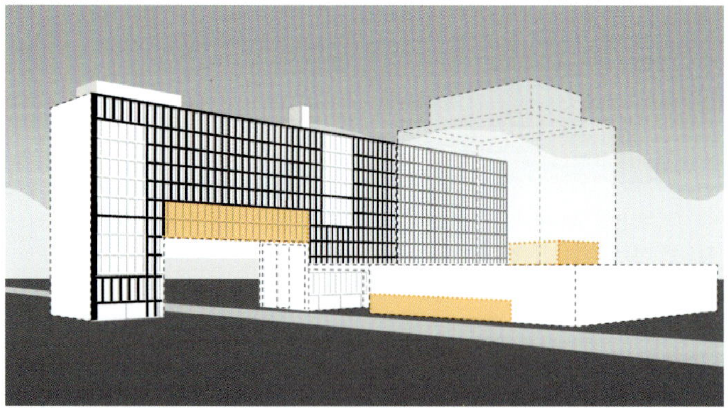

6

The strategic design moves were finally refined in diagrammatic form. The facade would be removed (1), and the slab block cut through (2). Houses within the slab would be defined (3), and a new facade added (4), while mini atria would serve each departmental house (5). Public rooms would be created at various places within the complex (6). A new Amsterdam canal bridge (7) would lead to the passage (8), which would give access to a suite of lecture theatres (9) and study landscapes. The facades of the point block (10) and its podium (11) would be replaced, and rooftop terraces added (12).

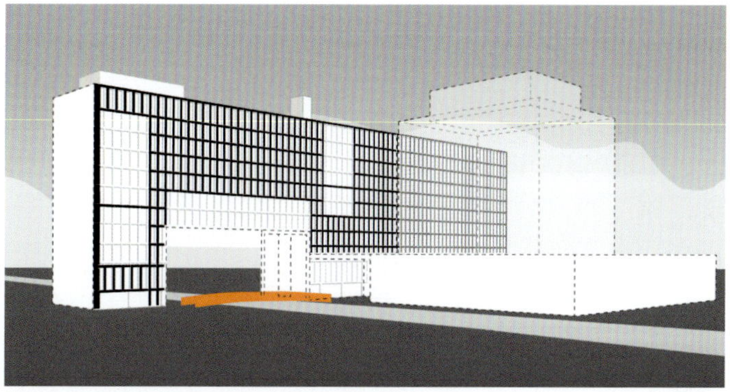
7

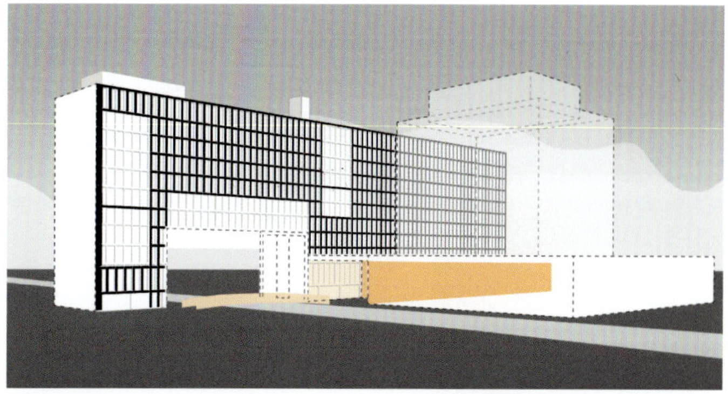
8

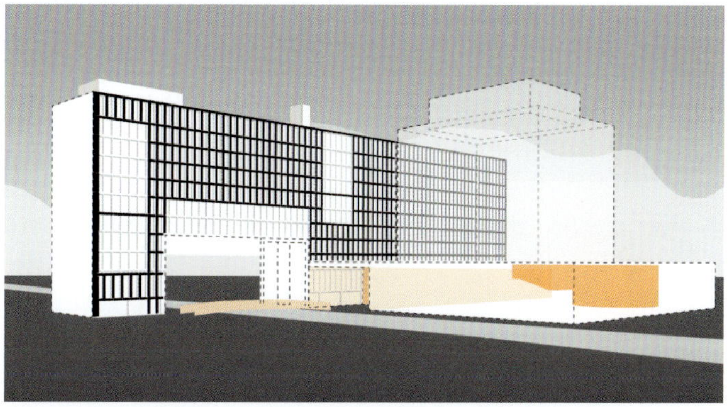
9

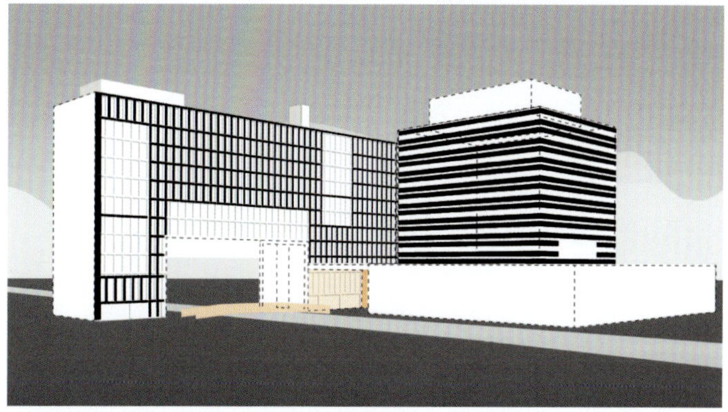
10

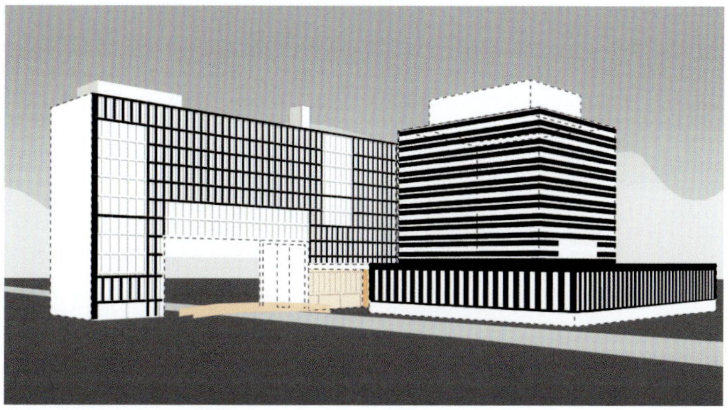
11

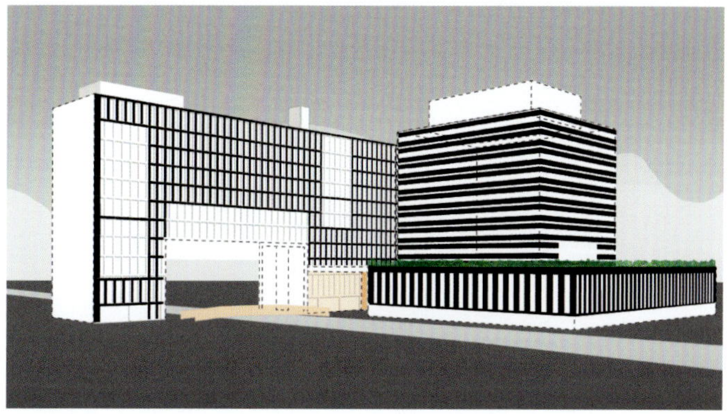
12

PHASES 4+5

APR 11–JAN 18

IN WHICH A BUILDING IS RECONNECTED TO CITY AND CAMPUS AND THE BRIEF MAKES A FEW FINAL EVOLUTIONS

IN WHICH THE SLAB BLOCK IS CUT AND REFURBISHED, AND PLAN B IS TEMPORARILY ADOPTED

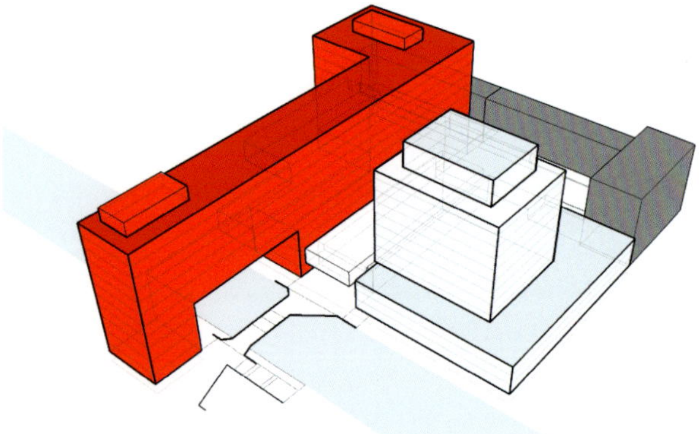

As the buildings were stripped out –
and certain elements demolished – the huge
mass and scale of the Gawronski blocks
became evident.

The installation of the huge box girder spanning the canal was an important moment in the cut process: once the new structure was built above it, the last of the original structure was removed from below.

The structure and scale of the block was most tangible in the skeleton of the new city room, slung below the girder.

The cut in progress, from September 2009 through to completion in 2014. The REC BC block was first stripped out and the part directly above the canal removed, leaving a small piled section below to act as a temporary work platform for the construction of the box girder as it was put into position. The section of block above the girder and spanning the canal was then rebuilt. Finally, the piled support was removed to reveal long views from the campus out into the city.

Work inside the structure took the form of a series of surgical interventions to carve out mini atria and stairwells within the existing slab.

With the cladding removed, the robust original structure was revealed. As its new envelope was added, a pattern of gloss and matt black, and clear glass, emerged.

With the addition of colour, the departmental houses began to be defined.

In the podium, large volumes were cut out for the new lecture theatres

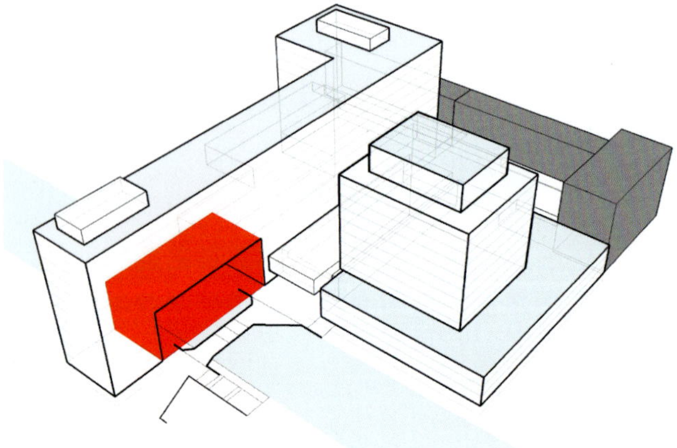

Construction progressed in two stages, with the slab block across the canal completing ahead of refurbishments to the passage and point block. A 'Plan B' was developed, with a temporary main entrance punched into the wall of the slab beneath the cut, so that the space above could be accessed while work continued.

Dear Simon,   Amsterdam 30.10.12

Few words only to tell you how right you were in insisting on "opening" the University to the neighbourhood.

The structural "sky-hook" stunt-work spanning the canal is quite impressive as is all the work in progress including the elegant facades.

All my best wishes to you,
as allways , yours

NICOLAS & JEAN-BAPTISTE RAGUENET
The Joust of the Watermen between the Pont Notre-Dame and the Pont au Change, 1756
Oil on canvas   Musée Carnavalet, Paris
Photo © Photothèque des Musées de la Ville de Paris

1012
Printed by The Beacon Press

The facades of the newly cut slab block have the same verticality as the original building, with colour defining the position of the various departmental houses within. Each of these is reached from its own mini atrium carved out of the main slab, clearly identifiable volumes within the larger volume. From the podium there are clear processional routes leading to the upper floors, encouraging users to navigate their journeys within by foot rather than by lift, as well as access to new lecture theatres.

Rather than a single central corridor, the slab block now has two, with departmental offices arranged along the glazed facades and shared amenities such as meeting rooms, tea points and bathrooms located in the central zone. A variety of more informal teaching and meeting areas, and study landscapes are also woven in to the flexible plan.

The huge city room, now renamed De Brug (The Bridge), has many different functions – meeting, eating, learning and socialising – and has views far out into the city along the Nieuwe Achtergracht. The same vistas are also now present at ground level, with the new cut opening up visual connections along the canal.

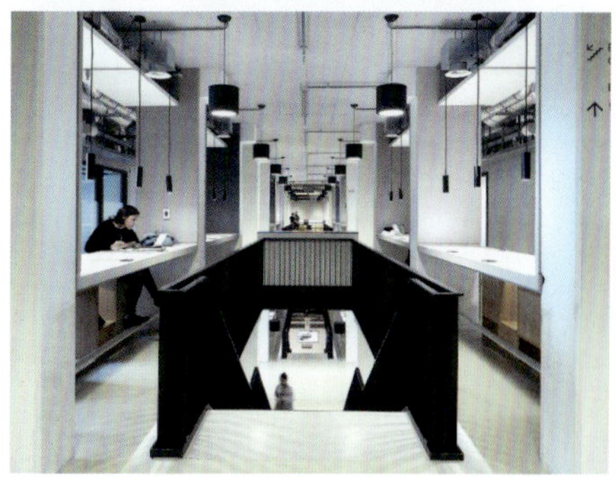

IN WHICH THE SHELL OF THE TOWER IS BUILT AND LATER, WITH THE PASSAGE, FITTED OUT AND COMPLETED

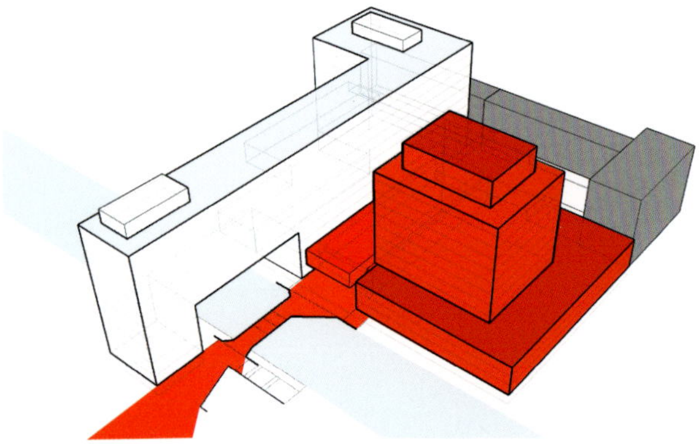

Point block A was stripped out within and the cladding removed to reveal the building's original skeleton.

Volumes for the new lecture theatres and tower atrium were carved out of the structure.

The new passage, connecting the slab and tower blocks and their podia, was constructed.

And even as the buildings were under construction, the brief continued to develop. The final evolution was an 'island', pierced by the structural columns of the passage, with a café space below and study space above.

The street facade of the tower's podium combines the reflective finish of the tower above with the vertical windows of the slab block. At ground level the facade is transparent while the upper levels have a combination of vision glazing and panels in a light grey-green tone to contrast with the stronger, darker silhouettes of the taller buildings.

The passage space gently guides people from their various modes and directions of arrival toward specific 'addresses' within the building. It is a sociable space, with access to several informal study landscapes, student societies and a catering kiosk. Below the passage, a lower-level concourse has secure parking space for thousands of bicycles.

The tower itself is home to the law faculty. Barbara Broekman's art piece in the seven-storey atrium is a collage of images of the judiciary taken from Western art history, and Biblical and mythological stories about the struggle between good and evil.

Specialist spaces such as a moot court are located within the tower alongside more generic lecture and seminar rooms, and staff offices. Study spaces in the fourth-floor law library overlook the canal. There are several catering facilities, and an external roof terrace sits on top of the podium base at third-floor level.

2
1

A&

C
C0.01, C0.02
C1.03, C1.04
BK, CK

ABC

BK
CK

A3-A10
DE VRIJE STUDENT
VIND JIJ HET ETEN IN DE KANTINE OOK TE DUUR?
KANTINEPETITIE.NL

C
C0.01, C0
C1.03, C1
BK, CK

C
De Brug
B, Eiland
A1-A2
B1-B2
C1-C2
De Brug
Eiland

PG

A7
A6

Enjoy
plant power
Good for you
Good for the planet

ABC
Welcome to the
Amsterdam
Roeterseiland

Coast to Coast

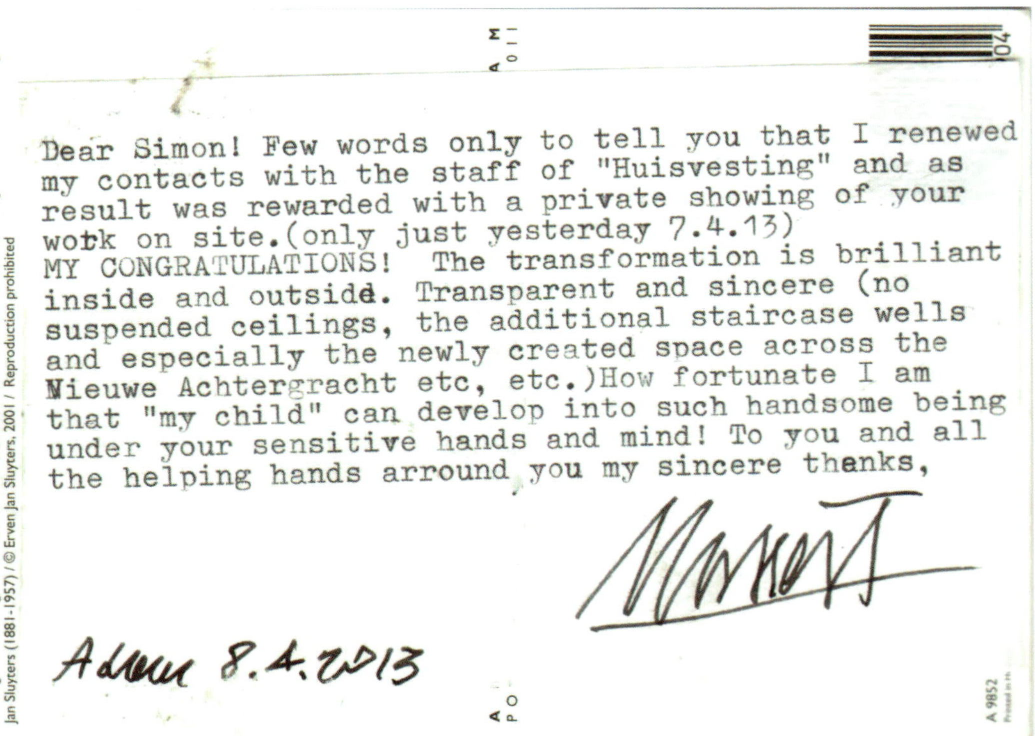

Dear Simon! Few words only to tell you that I renewed my contacts with the staff of "Huisvesting" and as result was rewarded with a private showing of your wotk on site.(only just yesterday 7.4.13)
MY CONGRATULATIONS! The transformation is brilliant inside and outsidd. Transparent and sincere (no suspended ceilings, the additional staircase wells and especially the newly created space across the Nieuwe Achtergracht etc, etc.)How fortunate I am that "my child" can develop into such handsome being under your sensitive hands and mind! To you and all the helping hands arround you my sincere thenks,

Adam 8.4.2013

Omslag van Wendingen over affiches van Nederlandse kunstenaars, maart 1923 / Lithografie naar een tekening van Jan Sluyters (1881-1957) / © Erven Jan Sluyters, 2001 / Reproduction prohibited

APPENDIX

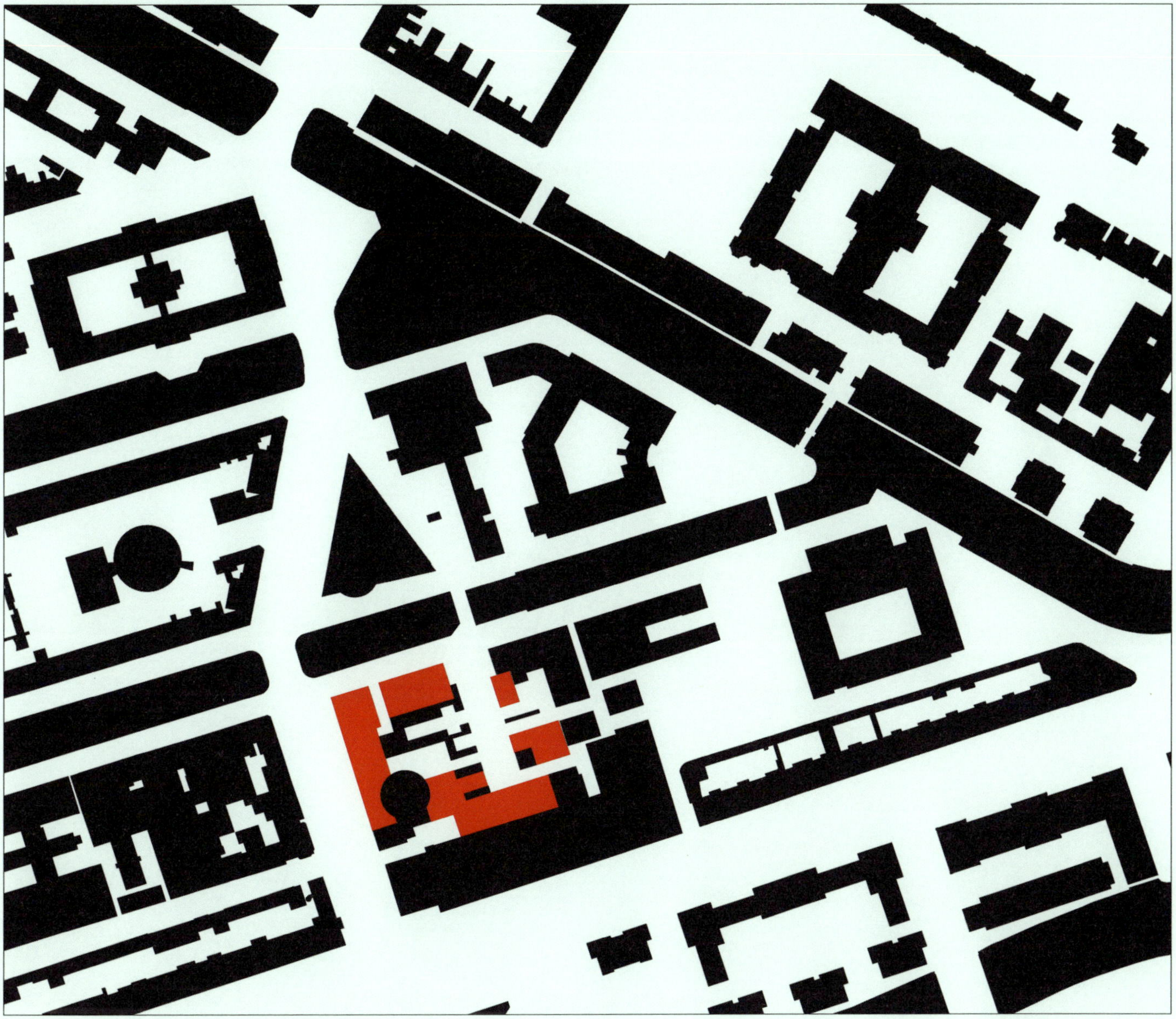

CITY PLAN

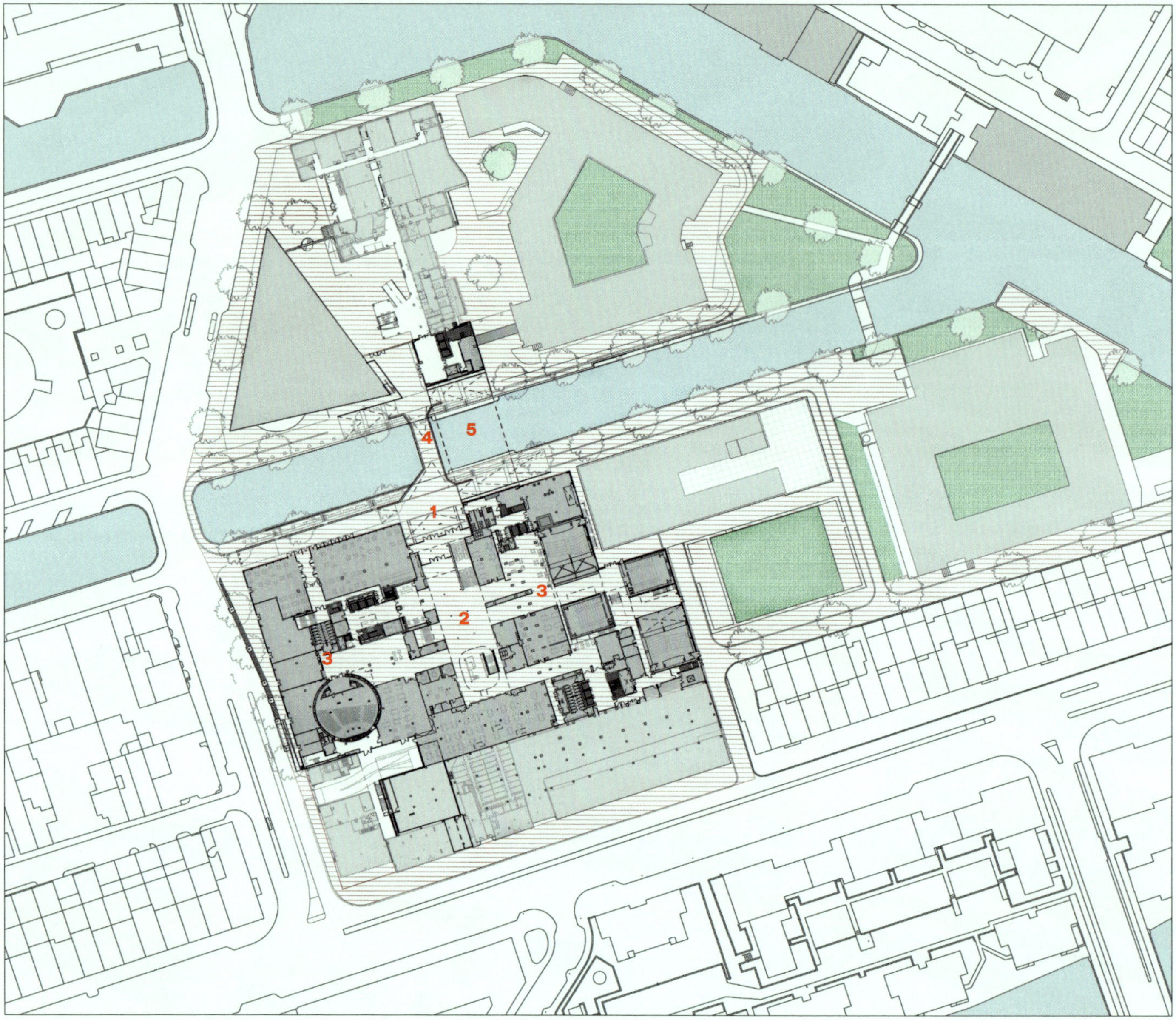

CAMPUS-LEVEL PLAN

1 Entrance to passage and basement cycle parking
2 Passage
3 Podium accommodation (seminar rooms, lecture theatres, study landscapes)
4 Bridge
5 Cut (slab block REC BC above)

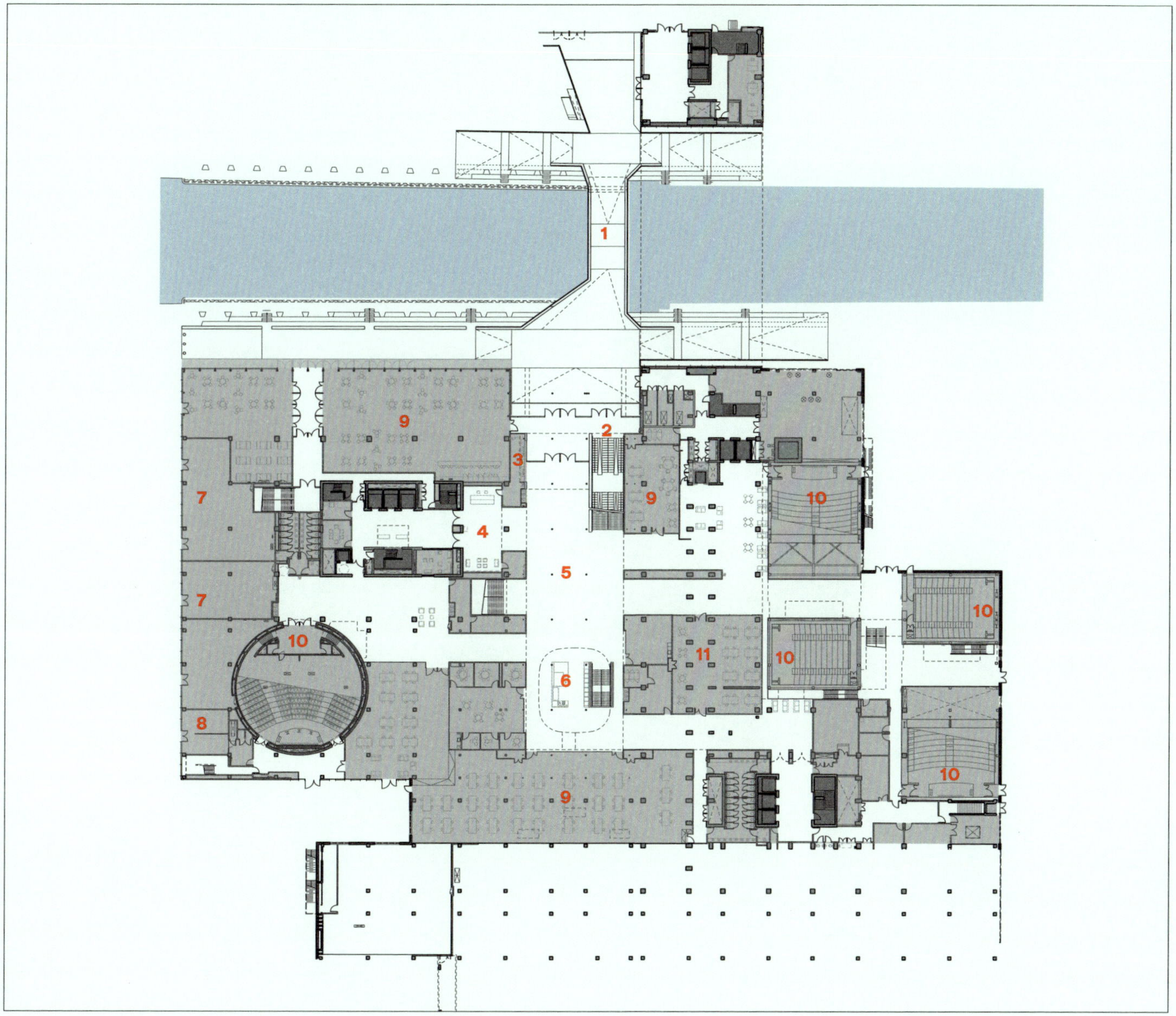

PASSAGE PLAN

1 Bridge
2 Entrance to basement cycle parking
3 General reception
4 Law faculty reception
5 Passage
6 Passage kiosk
7 Commercial units (onto Roetersstraat)
8 Pro bono law kiosk
9 Study landscapes
10 Lecture theatres
11 Student societies

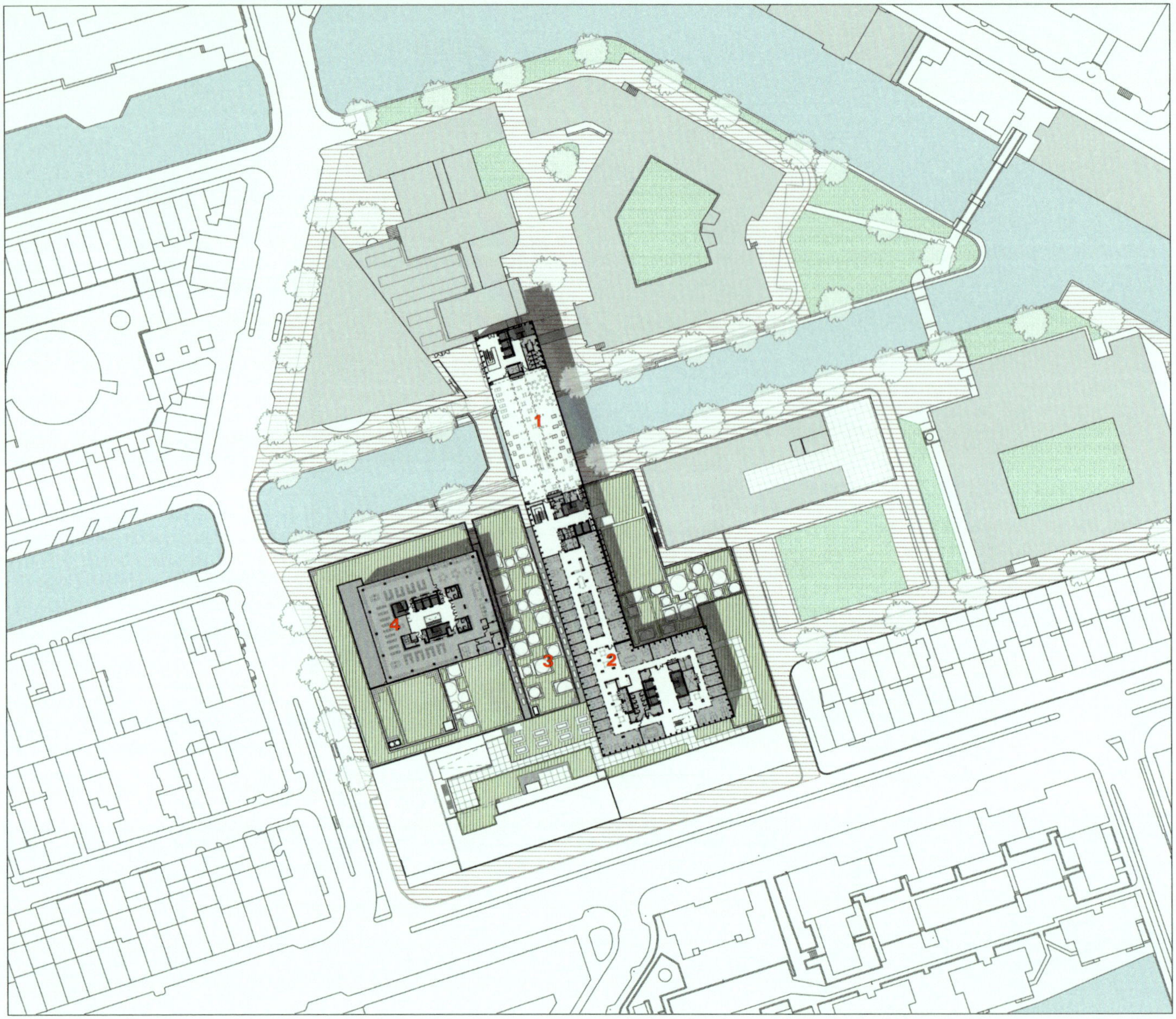

FOURTH-FLOOR PLAN

1 City room (Der Brug)
2 Departmental offices and tutorial rooms
3 Roof of passage
4 Law faculty library and study spaces

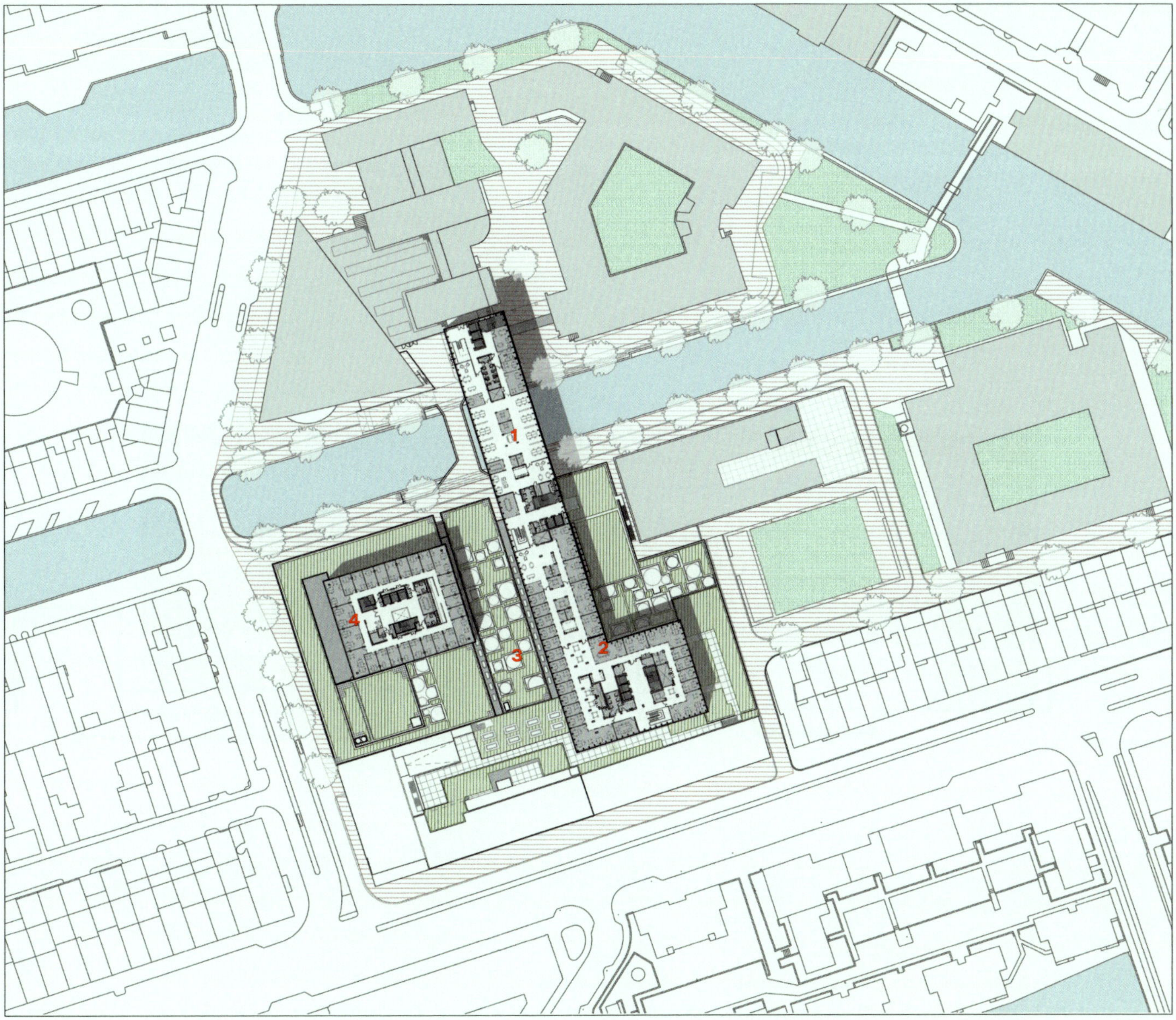

TYPICAL OFFICE FLOOR PLAN

1 Departmental study spaces
2 Departmental offices and tutorial rooms
3 Roof of passage
4 Law faculty staff offices

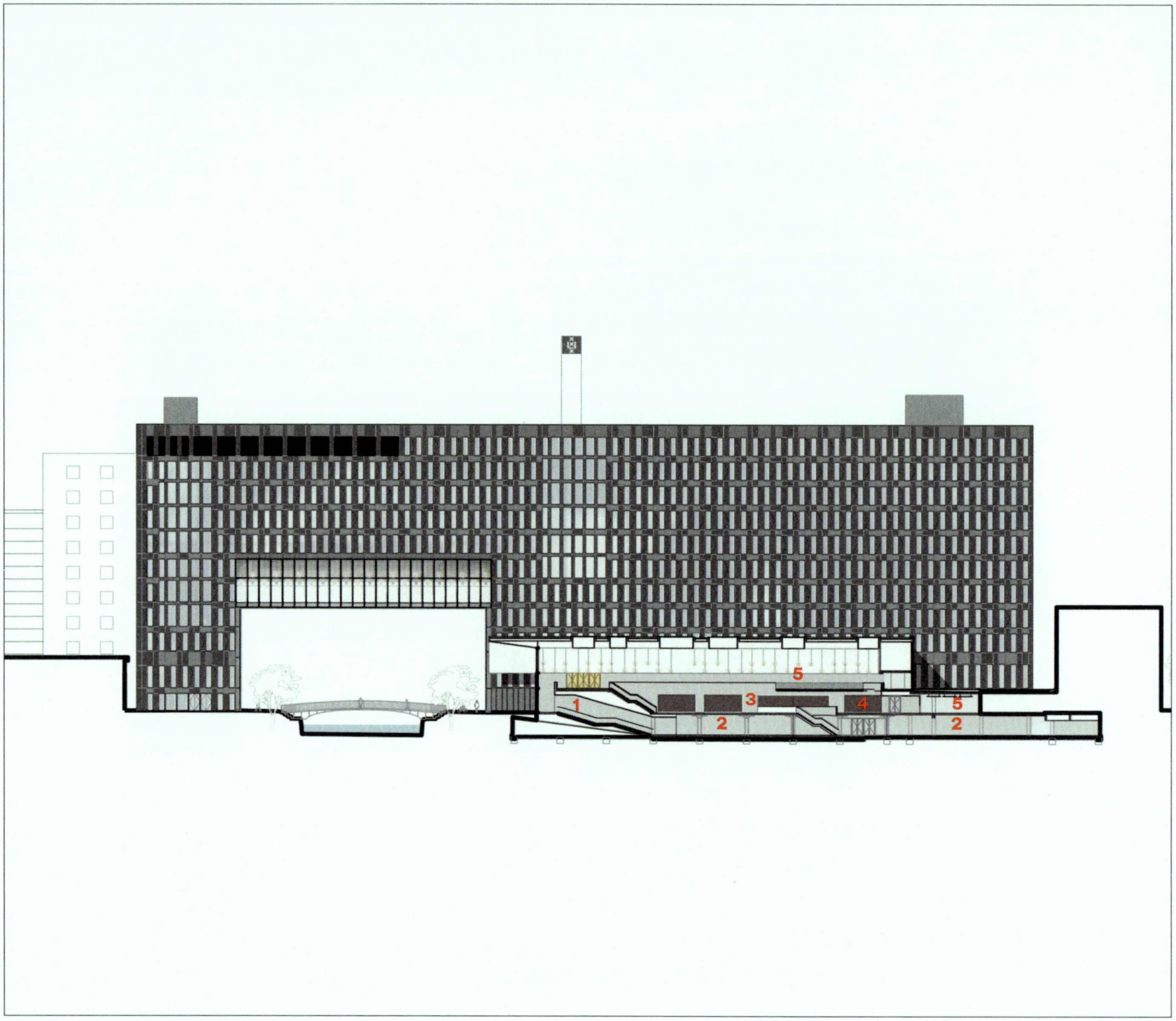

SECTION ALONG PASSAGE

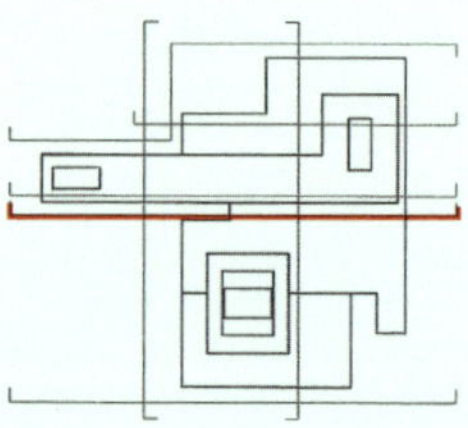

1 Ramp to cycle parking
2 Basement cycle parking
3 Passage
4 Passage kiosk
5 Study landscapes

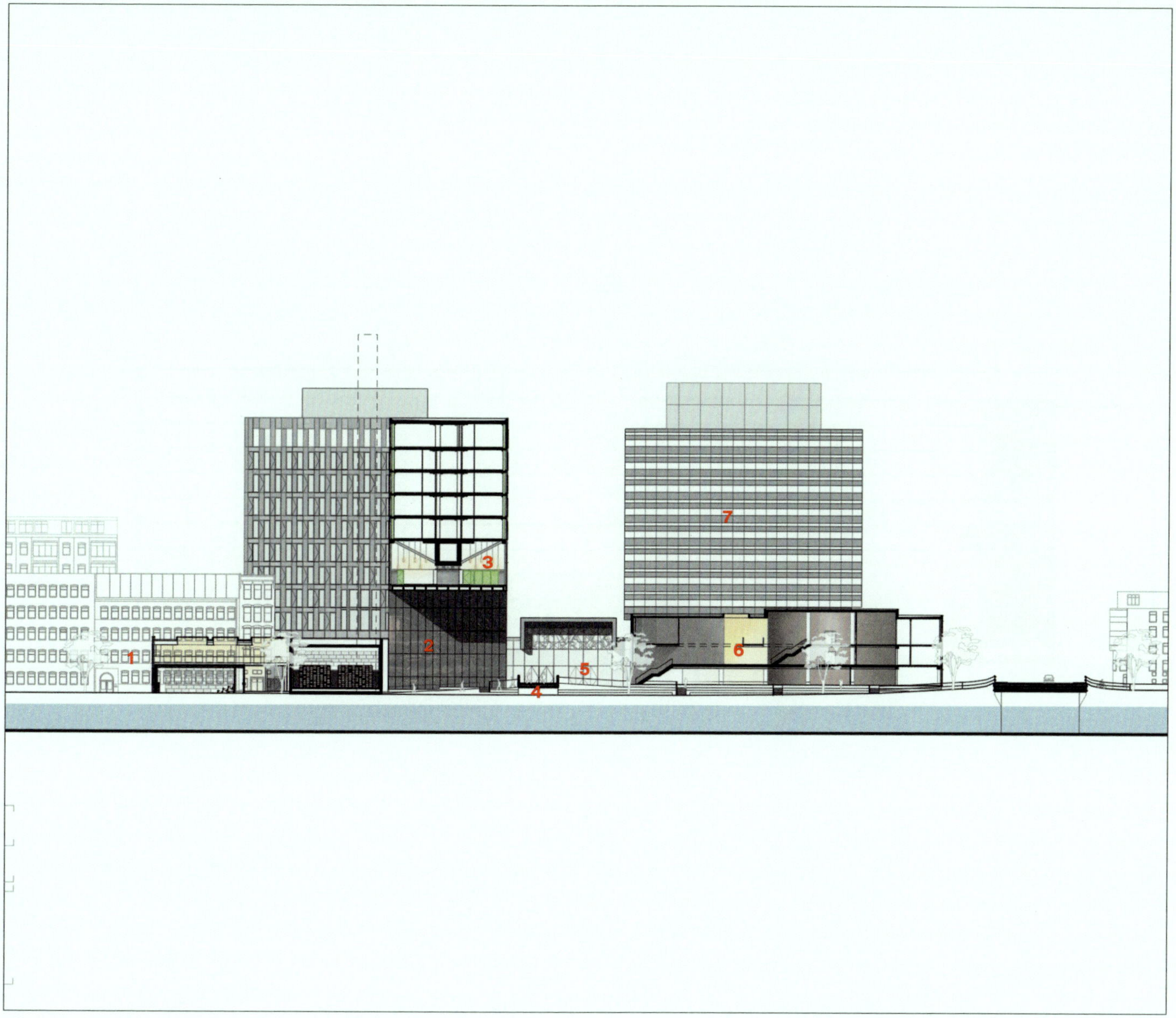

SECTION ALONG CANAL

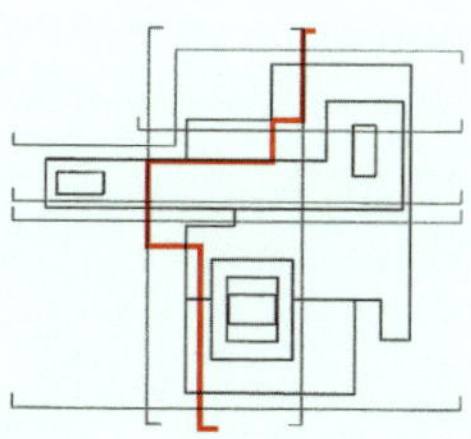

1 CREA
2 Cut
3 City room (and REC BC space above)
4 Bridge
5 Entrance to passage
6 Podium accommodation
7 REC A (law faculty)

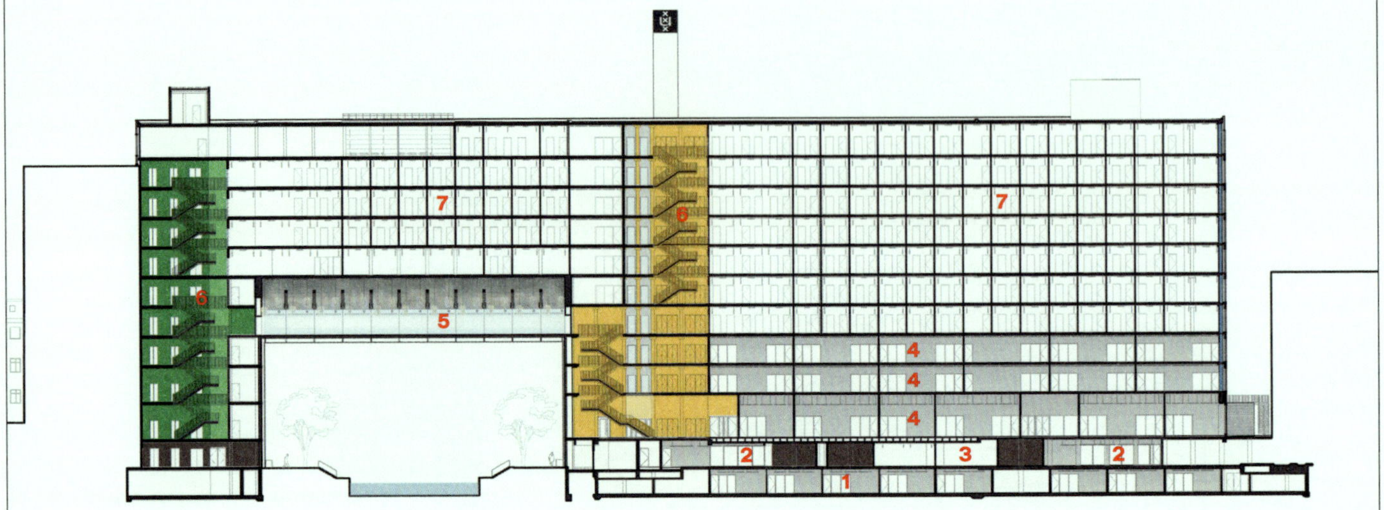

SECTION ALONG REC BC

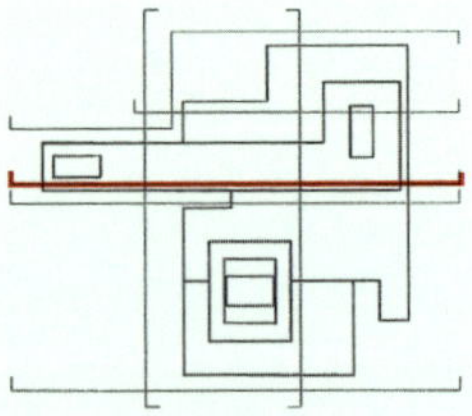

1 Cycle parking
2 Study landscapes
3 Student societies
4 Tutorial rooms
5 City room
6 Departmental atria
7 Departmental offices

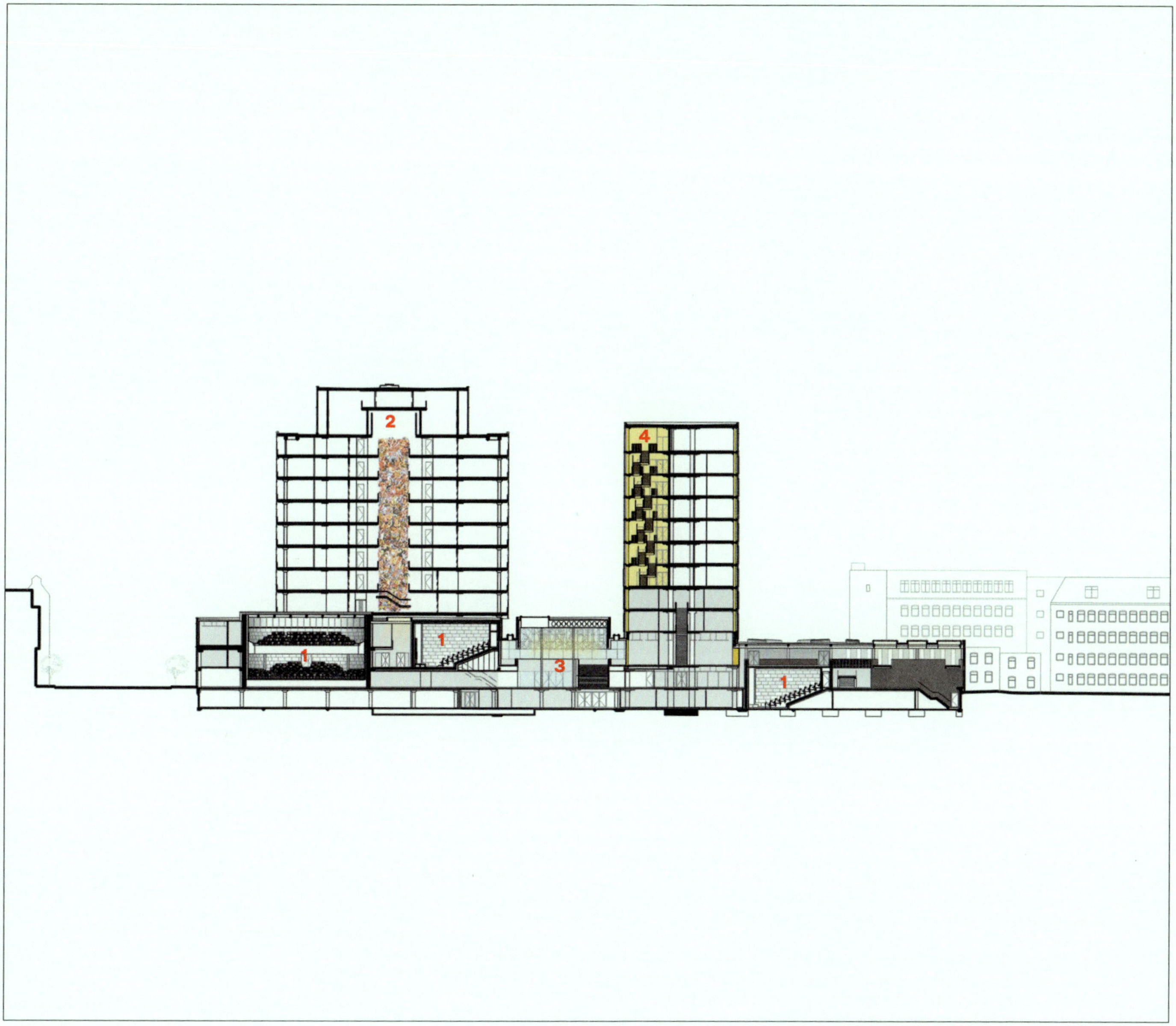

SECTION ACROSS REC ABCD

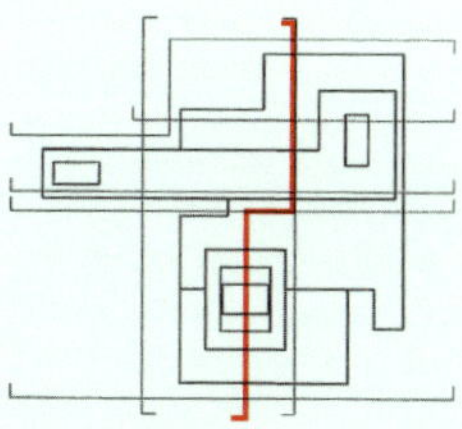

1 Lecture theatres
2 Law atrium
(with Barbara Broekman artwork)
3 Passage
4 REC BC stair and departmental atrium

TEAM AND CLIENTS

Client	University of Amsterdam	
Architect	Allford Hall Monaghan Morris	
Team	Simon Allford, Matt Allen, Big Bilski, Ming Chung, Paul Colfer, Daniel Cook, Ian Darlington, Emily Dukes, Ian Emmerson, Christina Fuchs, Jonathan Hall, Matt Hayward, Paul Jenkins, Matt Justice, Pilwon Kim, Poppy Kirkwood, Yuk Ming Lam, Ellie Mackenzie, Sarah McCartney, Barbara McGarry, Paul Monaghan, Peter Morris, Andrew Morrison, Steve Morton, David Potts, Louise Regan, Robert Romanis, Koen Schaballie, Clementine Seymour, Poppy Smith, Giulia Sonzogno, Aggie Szala, Morag Tait, Michael Taylor, Holli Thackray, Haydn Thomas, Benjamin Veyrac, Euan Watson, Rhys Winslade, Odette Olde Wolbers, Esther Worthington, Joe Wright	
Subconsultant architect	Phase I	ZZDP Architecten
Structural engineer	Pieters Bouwtechniek BV	
Services engineer	Ingenieursburo Linssen BV	
Building physics	LBP Sight	
Cladding consultant	IBS Consultants BV	
Central plant advisor	Deerns Raadgevende Ingenieurs BV	
Health and safety consultant	Adviesburo Nieman BV	
Project manager/cost advisor	Phase I	Royal HaskonigDHV
	Phase II	Aronsohn Management
Graphic designer	Hat-trick Design	
Interior design	Phase I offices	Fokkema & Partners Architecten
	Study landscapes	PUUR interieurarchitecten
Landscape architect	Inside Outside	
Masterplanner	Palmbout Urban Landscapes	

TEAM AND CLIENTS (CONTINUED)

Main contractor	Phase I	BAM Utiliteitsbouw
	Phase II	TBI Holdings B.V
Trade contractors	AKS Bouw BV, Heijmans, Kwakman, Licotec, Omnia	
Suppliers	Meinertz, Fagerhult, Germacell, Barrisol, Baswa acoustic, Ecophon, Bolidt, Lambri, Inteco, Corian, ZNR, Stretch design, Jansen	

FACTS AND FIGURES

Location	Amsterdam, The Netherlands	
Value	£84.5 million (Phases I and II)	
Start	Phase I	April 2011
	Phase II	November 2012
Completion	Phase I	March 2014
	Phase II	January 2018
Gross internal area (GIA)	Total	67,654 square metres
	Phase I	45,103 square metres
	Phase II	22, 551 square metres
Contract type	Phase I	two-stage negotiated traditional tender
	Phase II	design and build

IMAGE CREDITS

15 (top), 21	Amsterdam City Archive
15 (bottom)	with thanks to Norbert Gawronski
16-17	City of Amsterdam
18-19	Norbert Gawronski/Amsterdam City Archive
22	Palmbout Urban Landscapes
23	Los Angeles County Museum of Art, CA, USA/Bridgeman Images © ADAGP, Paris and DACS, London 2018
46-47, 69, 86-87, 96 (left)	Pieters Bouwtechniek BV
115	Inside Outside
116-117	with thanks to Barbara Broekman
All photography	Timothy Soar, Rob Parrish
All other models, images and drawings	Allford Hall Monaghan Morris
Disclaimer	All drawings, sketches and other photography by Allford Hall Monaghan Morris Every effort has been made to trace the copyright holders for the images used in this book and we apologise for any inadvertent errors or omissions. We are very happy to correct such oversights and incorporate any necessary changes in future editions.

020

Published
November 2019

Title
University of Amsterdam: a minigraph

Author
Allford Hall Monaghan Morris/
Simon Allford

ISBN
978-0-9934378-8-5

Design
Graphic Thought Facility

Print
Pureprint Group

Specification
220 × 220 mm, 224 pp
Typeset in Mercator
by Dick Dooijes (1959) /
Laurenz Brunner (2006/19), Source Type
Cover typeset in Instituut
by Irregular Type

FifthMan